Opening
Your Heart

Opening Your Heart

HOW TO ATTRACT MORE
LOVE INTO YOUR LIFE

Anne Jones

PIATKUS

Visit the Piatkus website!

Piatkus publishes a wide range of bestselling fiction and non-fiction, including books on health, mind, body & spirit, sex, self-help, cookery, biography and the paranormal.

If you want to:
- read descriptions of our popular titles
- buy our books over the internet
- take advantage of our special offers
- enter our monthly competition
- learn more about your favourite Piatkus authors

VISIT OUR WEBSITE AT: www.piatkus.co.uk

First published in Great Britain in 2007 by
Piatkus Books Ltd
5 Windmill Street, London W1T 2JA
email: info@piatkus.co.uk

ISBN 978 0 7499 2759 2

Text design by Briony Chappell
Edited by Steve Gove

This book has been printed on paper manufactured
with respect for the environment using wood from
managed sustainable resources

Printed and bound in Great Britain by
Antony Rowe Ltd, Chippenham, Wilts

CONTENTS

To the most generous and open hearted man I know – my husband Tony. Thank you, sweetheart, for your giving nature and your unconditional love.

ACKNOWLEDGEMENTS

To John for his brilliant advice and amazing wisdom – you are always proved right, John.

To my fellow travellers, the princesses, Harjeet, Tatiana, Pola, Sandra, Ines and Suseela – for making me realise I am a princess!

To Bishnu and his team for getting us into and out of Tibet more or less in one piece – a heartfelt thank you to the driver who brought me down the mountain and saved my life.

To my mother for her continual love and support of everything I do – you're my inspiration, Mousie.

To Tessie for looking after Penny, Tanya and Tony so that I can go on adventures of discovery and then have the time to write about them – you're my angel, Tessie.

To Gill Bailey and Helen Stanton, my editors at Piatkus, for your encouragement and guidance in helping me bring this book to fruition.

ONE

The Benefits of an Open Heart

I leant forward, listening intently to the words of the psychic. Having recently felt the call to start healing, I was desperate to hear what my destiny would be and where my healing would take me. My expectations were high, for the reader was internationally renowned and came highly recommended. She looked at her cards again, then looked up at me and smiled. 'Your healing powers are good,' she declared. 'But when your heart opens they will go from this' – she held her palms apart by about six inches – 'to this.' She stretched her arms wide open. I must say I felt a little affronted. My heart open – wasn't it open already? Didn't I love enough? I thought I was quite a caring person! As I left her room I pondered on her words. I took a little consolation that my healing would eventually become more effective, but it troubled me that my heart might seem closed.

I had this reading some twelve years ago but it's only been in the last couple of years that I have come to fully understand her message. My understanding came through that

An open heart lets in friends

powerful teacher, personal experience. I was led through a number of profound spiritual experiences which culminated in the opening of my heart. The results have changed my life dramatically and the benefits have been tremendous. I now understand the workings of our spiritual heart, the impact of heartache and heartbreak, the barriers we put up around our hearts. I have experienced the intense and life-changing effects that occur when we heal our hearts, bring down the barriers and open our hearts to receive love. I have helped hundreds of people through the process and seen them move through this beautiful and uplifting experience. Many have told me that they had a sense that they had been waiting for this for a long, long time. They embraced it with a feeling of excited anticipation, resulting in a sweet and emotional release.

SUE'S STORY

To give you an insight into the effect of opening up and receiving love, let me share with you the experience of Sue, a client of mine. Sue had been depressed for some years. Her mother, children and friends were extremely worried about her state of mind, as she had deteriorated to the point where she talked constantly of suicide. She told me of her unhappy childhood with a drunken and abusive father who was subsequently replaced by an equally drunken and abusive stepfather. I asked her if she had ever felt good, whether anything had made her feel happy or contented. She thought about this and said there was an occasion when she was quite small, about four years old, standing in the rain watching the raindrops falling into a puddle. She said this memory had brought back to her a

An open heart lets in healing

sense of calm and peace. I asked her if there was any one event in her life that had caused her great sorrow and she told me that she had lost her first child, a boy. She cried as she recalled the loss and pain caused by his death. She was obviously still nursing a broken heart and she said she felt guilty for his passing.

Low self-esteem, guilt, grief and a traumatic relationship with her father had created a disastrous cocktail which had resulted in her sad and unhappy state of mind. She was currently separated from her husband but had three children that she loved. Her mother too was very caring and loving, but she was unable to open in order to receive and enjoy her mother's love or that of her children – her heart was too painful, and deep down she just didn't believe that she deserved love or happiness.

I gently took her through a healing session, focusing particularly on her heartache. She tentatively allowed her heart to open, and little by little let go of the dark and heavy energy of grief and guilt that she held deep inside her. As she opened up she accepted the love that I was sending to her for her healing. I could feel the transformation taking place as her energy became lighter and lighter. She started smiling and when she eventually opened her eyes they sparkled – she looked around her as though she was in a different place. She said she felt lighter, much lighter, and yes, happy – a feeling that she hadn't experienced for as long as she could remember.

Sue's experience is typical of many of the people I have helped to let go their sadness, open their hearts and receive love. Let's look first at some of the circumstances that result in being closed down and see if they apply to you.

An open heart lets in comfort

IS YOUR HEART CLOSED?

A closed heart can affect you in many ways. In the most extreme circumstances it will mean that you are unable to allow anyone to get close to you. You will be unable to accept love in any form. You will be lonely and isolated. You will be unable to feel compassion and empathy for others, which will further isolate you. You will find any form of relationship difficult and the outcome will be a lonely and sad life. Like Sue, you may be feeling depressed. Her case was extreme, but there are many of us who have closed down our hearts to some degree. We may experience any of these emotions and situations:

✧ a feeling of distance between you and those closest in your life

✧ fear of being rejected

✧ a constant heavy feeling in your chest, along with a deep inner sadness

✧ feeling depressed and low in spirit and energy

✧ feeling overwhelmed by life

✧ attracting people who are damaged emotionally

✧ always creating tempestuous relationships

✧ constant misunderstandings with those close to you at home or work

✧ fear of being alone

✧ fear that others will not be accepting

✧ lack of confidence

An open heart lets in fun

✧ feeling victimised

✧ low self-esteem and lack of self-appreciation

✧ difficulty in seeing the roses, let alone smelling them

✧ difficulty in finding a suitable partner

✧ a feeling that life is a battle

✧ a constant feeling of anger in the background of your life

✧ a constant feeling of anxiety

✧ a feeling that there must be more to life

✧ feeling guilty

✧ difficulty finding the right work or a job that totally suits you

✧ difficulty either in making money or holding on to it

✧ feeling hollow inside – an emptiness that is difficult to fill

✧ waking up feeling tetchy and irritable before anyone has even spoken to you

✧ feeling convinced that there is nobody out there for you

✧ feeling weepy for no apparent reason

✧ feeling that you will never fall in love again

Do you think any of these apply to you? I would be very surprised if you didn't, for most people are suffering from some form of lack of love. These are just some of the manifestations of lack of love or painful past experiences with love.

An open heart lets in appreciation

The emotions and feelings that are created as a direct result of lack of love, or inability to give love either to others or yourself, will have ramifications deep in your daily life. They will affect your happiness and capacity for inner peace. They will result in attitudes to life and behaviour patterns that will most often exacerbate the situation and make you unhappy, disillusioned with life and frustrated – knowing there is more but unsure and unaware of how to claim it.

Throughout this book I will be looking at all these conditions and more, and I will suggest ways that you can relieve and heal them, for they are all forms of pain coming from a wounded heart. I will help you heal the heartache, heartbreak and guilt that act as barriers stopping love coming into your life.

Love is essential for a rich, fulfilling, happy life. Lack of love in any degree can affect the way you see yourself and your world. It affects your perception of your life. It limits your ability to live life to its fullest. Once your heart is open you will find your life enriched – not only will your perspective on what is going on around you change, but also you will find you attract more uplifting experiences and people. Things will start to work for you and your life will become more bountiful. Every aspect of your life will improve: work, social, home, family.

Heart opening is a healing of the heart. It is an opportunity to heal and let go the pain from past experiences, to forgive people who have hurt you and to heal old grief.

Some of the scars and damage to your emotional heart may be very old, going back to childhood and beyond. So it can take time to tend and nurse it back to full health. We will look at all the experiences that can cause damage, and the results that can make your life difficult or miserable now. We will work with abandonment, grief, abuse – both physical and

An open heart lets in peace

emotional – spiritual disillusionment and guilt. All of these are significant causes of heart damage. We will look at ways you can release your connections to past trauma and live fully today. Where you are still in situations that cause you distress, we will look at ways you can handle and avoid the hurt. You can repair and rebuild, strengthening your emotional heart so that you can live a full and enjoyable life.

Once your heart is open you can flood yourself and your life with love. You can become discerning, choose unconditional love rather than emotions like possessiveness and control that disguise themselves as love. Love is limitless and there is an infinite supply, so let's find ways for you to get your share – and more! Does that sound good?

THE BENEFITS OF AN OPEN HEART

Let's now look at some of the benefits of a healed and open heart that allows you to make a constant and open connection to the love that life can offer:

✦ You will attract friendly and supportive people into your life.

✦ You will start to feel more vital and energised.

✦ You will see and appreciate your blessings and the good things of life.

✦ You will see the positive side of situations and people.

✦ You will notice people smiling at you and being kinder.

✦ You will find yourself laughing more easily.

An open heart lets in confidence

✧ You will feel lighter and uplifted.

✧ Your luck will seem to change – good things will start to happen.

✧ Your relationships will seem easier and less of a struggle.

✧ You will find it easier to find work that fulfils you.

✧ You will attract love in every form, from romance to respect.

✧ Your finances may improve.

✧ You will feel more at peace within, and calmer.

✧ Crises and dramas may be healed and dealt with more easily.

✧ Your work will seem less of a burden.

✧ You will feel more spiritual and closer to God.

✧ It will be easier to communicate your feelings.

✧ Life will become a pleasure rather than a struggle.

These are just some of the changes that people tell me they have experienced once their hearts have opened.

Of course, any major transformation requires the will to change, the determination to work on your attitudes, emotions and perception of life – you will want to deeply and sincerely feel the need to change. I will assist you with techniques and processes that I have found helpful for letting go old pent-up emotions, for forgiving and letting go the past and seeing yourself and others in a different light. However, the work is yours, and the will and determination

An open heart lets in family

will be yours. But the rewards are great and I know you will find the journey worthwhile.

If you decide to move forward and make these changes, to undertake this repair work, then I would like to emphasise something right now. *You are not 'bad' if your heart is closed*. It doesn't even mean you cannot give love – but rather that you are unable to receive it. I am not asking you to beat yourself up for the things that you have or haven't done in the past. This is about taking a long, cool look at the present and deciding to change things for the better – for yourself and subsequently all those around you. So, if you realise that there is work to be done, don't start feeling guilty or resentful. Just roll up your metaphysical sleeves and let's get down to work.

I will start by taking you on my own personal journey – for without this I would not have understood and experienced how wonderful the release can be. I will then share my understanding of love and the emotional goal that we are seeking – a life filled with love. I will share my perceptions of unconditional love; the ultimate form of love that can change your life. We will see what causes our hearts to break and why the loss of love can be so painful. Next we will reach the explanation of how you can open your own heart to receive love. Once your heart is open you can heal the wounds that caused the closure by letting go of the past. We will then look at how you can repair and improve your current relationships, making them more fulfilling and loving. Finally we will look at ways that you can create and attract new loving relationships – in fact fill your life with love and romance!

Throughout this book I will be continually focusing on the greatest and most powerful of your emotions: LOVE. How does that sound to you? I get excited whenever I think

An open heart lets in the sun

about the transformation that more love can make for anyone, whether you are single, divorced, married, living with someone or alone after a lifetime of sharing. Everyone can have more love – and once you know how, it's really not that difficult. There is an infinite amount of love to be claimed in the universe – why shouldn't you get your share?

So first I'll tell you the story of how my heart was opened and the help I had from angels and the wise ones of the spirit world. I will share how this has changed my life and affected the way I feel and work. At the time of these experiences my life, just like every woman's, was a mixture of practical and domestic chores, work responsibilities, and social time with family and friends. It was with this background that I received these spiritual insights and experiences, all of which affected my ability to love. They released the pent-up emotions that I had held down for years, even lifetimes; they healed pain and wounds held in my heart; they helped magnify the energies that I work with and allowed a greater flow of universal love for healing; they opened my heart and increased my capacity to give and receive love. Considering that everyone I know would like more love – and certainly the world needs more love – I think it worth sharing . . .

We have a busy time ahead, so are you ready? If you want more love in your life then come with me on this journey – let's go.

An open heart lets in friends

TWO
My Heart Opening

I started practising healing some years ago following a wake-up call from my grandmother who had spoken to me one day from spirit. This wake-up call came to me like a powerful thought with sound, for I could hear my grandmother's voice and sense her without seeing her. She had guided me to start healing that day and since then I have evolved a form of healing that focuses on the root cause of the problems that materialise as emotional, mental or physical pain. The origins are often held deep in a person's consciousness and energy field as imprints from past experiences either in this lifetime or in previous soul lives. These imprints often wound the spiritual heart and soul deeply, and can seriously affect a person's happiness, health and general wellbeing.

Over the last twelve years I have travelled extensively, giving seminars and healing sessions. Occasionally through my travels I have received a new gift or insight into another facet of healing. My own heart opening began during a visit to Singapore in 2001 with a gift – another personal message, though this time not from my grandmother. I was giving a healing session to Suseela, herself a young teacher and healer. As the session ended she opened her eyes and smiled. 'I feel

An open heart lets in respect

great – I saw my spirit guide and I have a message for you. We need to go to the Kwan Yin temple nearby where she has something important to tell you.' Kwan Yin is the Buddhist goddess of mercy. She radiates an amazing energy of love and compassion; she is my favourite of the Buddhist deities.

So the next day we went together to the Kwan Yin temple. Suseela has the ability to connect to loving spiritual forces and she can be a conduit for the words of Kwan Yin; simply by closing her eyes and focusing on Kwan Yin she surrenders her voice to the spiritual master who then gives her message of guidance and love. In précis she told me that my heart was about to start opening, which would herald a new spiritual phase in my life. The opening would start in Singapore but it was important for me to visit Tibet, where a major development would occur beside a river surrounded by mountains. I would also visit a cave in a mountainside that would affect me deeply. She also gave me her blessings which felt like being held in a warm embrace.

As I listened to these words I experienced the shimmering energy that I feel when I hear the truth. A positive shiver of energy went through me and I knew the message was absolutely genuine. And despite some misgivings about travelling to Tibet, I knew that I had to go!

FORGIVING GOD

I was giving a seminar the following day and one of the participants approached me. She had recently been with Sandra Gonzalez, a friend of mine who had taken a group on the old Inca trail to Machu Picchu in Peru. Sandra knew she would be meeting me in Singapore and had given her a gift for me. It was an enamelled silver pendant depicting

An open heart lets in strength

the head of an Inca god. I was thrilled and immediately put it on.

An hour later I started to get tiny cramps in my chest. Through the day these developed into quite painful spasms. I felt a little concerned, so I called a psychic friend who told me that my heart centre was beginning to open. The Incan pendant was the catalyst, due to an experience I had had in a past life. I was thrilled. It had started!

Later that day I had some personal quiet time and during a meditation I felt this pendant reconnect me to a past life where I had lived in Peru. I saw myself as a priest for a South American civilisation – most likely the Incas. I visualised myself standing on a hill overlooking our land, watching an army of Spanish conquistadores approaching. I watched them as they slaughtered my people, all the while holding aloft a huge cross that bore a figure of Jesus. My heart hardened to the God of the invaders before I too died, stabbed in the chest with a spear.

I now became aware of the reason my heart was closed. The experience of seeing destruction and death brought about in God's name had left me angry with him. The emotions that we hold at the time of death can have long-term effects on following lifetimes, and my spirit guides told me my heart was blocked by bitterness. To clear the pain I would need to forgive God and give him my heart.

A few days later I flew from Singapore to Kuala Lumpur, in Malaysia, and my thoughts returned to the message to forgive God. It dawned upon me that my 'problem with God' was of my own making. Though his love is infinite and continual, I had put up a barrier that stopped me receiving his love. This enlightening insight released my bitterness and in that moment I was overcome with waves of love and gratitude towards God. I had a vision in which I handed

An open heart lets in compassion

over my heart to two beautiful etheric hands that reached out to me. My heart immediately turned to gold and was returned to me.

The plane landed with me crying my heart out. I opened my eyes, mopped myself up and started to giggle. What did I look like? And what were my travelling companions thinking of this weird woman weeping and laughing? Unfortunately, we can't always choose where we have our spiritual moments!

A few months later, on a visit to Hong Kong, I shared Kwan Yin's message and my intention to travel to Tibet with friends and before I knew it we had become a group of six. Plans were made, dates were set and the next step in my journey was set in motion.

TIBET

Eventually it was time for our trip. I flew to join my friends from Hong Kong in Kathmandu, Nepal. From there we made our way by bus to our first stop, a small hotel close to the border of Tibet. The following morning we crossed the 'Friendship Bridge' over a steep gorge into Tibet and travelled through mountain passes into the foothills of the Himalayas. We were transported by land cruiser up the winding mountain roads, and despite slipping and sliding on the muddy tracks we made it to our night's campsite, our first taste of sleeping in a tent in the wilds of Tibet.

That night I couldn't sleep, I had a headache and nausea. I didn't realise it at the time, but I was suffering the early stages of altitude sickness. We were already at 3,000 metres, and in just three days I had travelled from England, via Dubai at sea level to Kathmandu and then on to the Tibetan plateau.

An open heart lets in tolerance

We continued our journey up rocky passes and through wide open valleys, with the magnificent snow-topped peaks of the Himalayas constantly on the skyline as the trail took us ever higher. But by now my head was starting to throb alarmingly. I was frequently sick and I felt awful. By the time we reached 5,000 metres, the height of the Everest base camp, I was obviously suffering severe altitude sickness. We stayed that night in a guest house. My head was splitting and throughout the night I was almost delirious. By the morning I felt I was going to die.

At that point it was decided that we had to go down to a safer altitude. We stopped more than once for me to be sick and on one such occasion I saw blood on my hand-kerchief. I showed it to my driver. Immediately he strapped me in and set off, speeding down the mountain passes at breakneck speed as I fell in and out of consciousness.

We arrived back at the town of Nyalam at a safer 3,750 metres and booked into a hotel. At the lower altitude I recov-ered quite quickly, but my close brush with death left me unsettled, vulnerable and very weak.

The next day, though I still felt weak, we ventured out to a small temple in a nearby Tibetan village. This was our first close look at a village; all the buildings were made from bricks of mud and straw-dried yak dung. Yak dung is also burnt on the cooking fires, which, as in the mountain villages of Nepal, are perilously positioned in the centre of the houses so that the smoke escapes through a hole in the roof. It is not unusual for children to fall on these open fires, and in the village I saw a youngster with his face badly burnt; to my horror his wounds were still weeping. But apparently this is a common sight. There is little money to spare for even basic health care in the villages. The sight of his poor burnt face disturbed me and I gave him money to pay for

An open heart lets in joy

medication and then continued on with my journey to the temple, not realising that the plight of this little lad would come back to haunt me later.

In the temple I meditated on my close encounter with death. I thanked God for my life. The response was a clear message – I should appreciate and value my good fortune. I had been working full on over the last few years with little time to enjoy my family and home. I promised myself to take more time to enjoy my life. There is nothing like a brush with death to make us appreciate life and our blessings.

A HEART ATTACK?

That day we decided to leave our hotel and moved down the valley to find a beautiful campsite beside a river. The girls gathered in the communal dining tent and, still feeling a little wobbly, I went to my tent to sleep. As I lay there I felt a tightening in my chest. It developed into a pain that grew stronger and stronger until I felt my chest would burst. The pains started to shoot from the centre of my chest like star bursts. Could it be a heart attack? But we were miles from support, with no doctors or hospitals nearby.

Feeling very, very scared I joined the girls. They tried to calm me and I closed my eyes. Immediately, I recalled the little boy in the village with his weeping wounds. My heart filled to bursting with emotion and I cried and cried as I thought of this young lad without even a tissue to wipe his face. Waves of compassion and love flowed from my heart, to him and all children in the world in need of love and care. Gradually as I cried, the pain dispersed and I was filled with strength and peace. Strength because I knew that somehow, some day I would do something to help; peace

An open heart lets in laughter

because I had released something that had been bottled up within me for a very long time.

I realise now that I had put barriers up to my heart – my emotional and spiritual heart, the energy centre found in the middle of our chest. The sight of the little boy and his poor burnt face had brought these barriers down and allowed my heart to open with compassion. Typically, we find that other people's extreme circumstances and pain are just too much to bear and we look away, even hardening our hearts to prevent the pain affecting us – I know I certainly did. At this time I was vulnerable and weak after my sickness and unable to avoid the feelings the little lad had touched. I have to say I have never been the same since – it was one of life's defining moments, I suppose.

Soon after this trip I met Douglas McLaren, who had started a charity in Nepal bringing basic health care to the mountain villages and showing the villagers how to build enclosed fires for cooking. It was great synchronicity – he showed me a way to help prevent horrendous burn injuries like those suffered by the little boy I'd met. Since my visit to Tibet my healing work has become more and more effective. And it was there, just as predicted by Kwan Yin, that the opening of my heart had started – beside a river and surrounded by great soaring peaks of mountains. Yet although the experience was profound and the resulting benefits tangible, this did not turn out to be the extent of my heart opening.

INDIA

A year later my friends and I decided to go on another 'spiritual holiday', this time to India. We decided that this time there would be no tents and no yaks – we would stay

An open heart lets in magic

in the best hotels we could afford. We found a charming old hotel in the French quarter of Pondicherry, situated on the south-eastern coast of India. In meditation Kwan Yin told me I would have a major transformation somewhere in India, leaving me to follow my intuition as to where to visit. Even before we arrived in India my heart centre was throbbing and I kept bursting into tears. I knew it meant a further emotional shift was beginning.

The first morning I woke with a surprising fixation – I needed to visit a Catholic church. How bizarre to visit India and choose to go to a church! However, Kwan Yin had told me to follow my own guidance, so we found one of the four Catholic churches in Pondicherry built during French colonial rule. As we entered I felt the need to sit quietly in a pew and meditate. It felt a little strange – I sat beneath a wooden statue of Mother Mary, who wore a string of Christmas lights around her head. Jesus looked on, his sacred heart pulsing a red glow from a light bulb in his chest. Despite the solemn atmosphere of the church I couldn't prevent myself smiling at these rather outrageous statues. I was still a little weepy so I clutched a box of tissues. As it turned out, I was going to need them. Over the four days we stayed in Pondicherry, I was to receive in the four churches some vital messages and undergo a powerful spiritual experience. Each day more unfolded for me but for ease of reading I will recount it as a continuous sequence.

ARCHANGEL RAPHAEL

I closed my eyes and relaxed, and into my inner vision came the spirit guides with whom I normally communicate in meditation; they were standing looking at me and smiling. They said they were leaving me for a week or two and waved goodbye. I was devastated; I felt abandoned and very lonely. I began to cry and reached for the tissues. I was dropping into the deepest gloom when into my inner vision an angel appeared. I recognised her as Archangel Raphael, the angel of healing. She smiled and put out her hands in welcome. She told me she was about to lead me on a journey within myself. My spirit guides had left to avoid me being distracted and connecting externally to spirit. I felt comforted and reassured to have her by my side as she led me forward. You may be personally affected by some of the magical, and in some cases shocking, revelations, sights and events I experienced and which I am about to share.

THE FIRST CHAMBER OF THE HEART

Raphael and I approached a door. She told me to push it open and I stepped into a chamber filled with a pink glow. In the centre a candle flame burned, filling the room with translucent light. She explained that this was my personal heart chamber, the first chamber of my heart centre. It felt good and uplifting, and she explained that this was the source of the love that I give to others. She asked me to spend some time there and absorb the love – in other words, receive for myself the love that I give out. As I complied, I felt amazing energy wash through me – so strong that again I started to weep, but this time with the magic of love and how effective it is to comfort. I smiled as a warm cosy glow spread through me. I looked around this beautiful place and saw family and friends from the past and present – in fact everyone I had let into my heart. They held out their arms to make me welcome, their love so powerful it was almost tangible.

Raphael stood in front of me to the left and now introduced me to three other angels. Ahead, to my right, stood

An open heart lets in empathy

Archangel Gabriel, behind me to the left was Archangel Uriel and behind me on my right shoulder was Archangel Michael.

These magnificent archangels have specific roles which I now realise were relevant to my experiences — although at the time I was completely overawed by their presence. Archangel Raphael is the guardian of healing. Archangel Gabriel is the guardian of hope, relationships, love and the heart. Archangel Uriel is the guardian of transformation; her name means 'Light of God'. Archangel Michael is the guardian of world peace, of protection.

They led me through the chamber to the far side, to a closed door which looked as though it hadn't been opened for eons. It was barricaded by a number of ancient planks, bolts and locks. Raphael informed me that I had a choice at this stage. I could stay where I was and leave the door barricaded; all would be well but I wouldn't advance or spiritually develop further. Or I could take down these barriers and move forward through the door to the unknown.

I felt extremely anxious and my heart beat furiously — although I didn't know why, for I was consciously unaware what lay behind the door. However, I couldn't contemplate staying stuck in the same place and not allowing myself to develop. How awful to spend the rest of my life not knowing what I could have achieved! No, staying still wasn't an option, despite my fear of what lay in wait for me. The angels helped me as I pulled down the bars on the door and broke through the locks and chains.

THE SECOND CHAMBER OF THE HEART

Eventually the door was ready to open and again I was asked if I wanted to go forward. 'Yes,' I responded emphatically. I

An open heart lets in serenity

pushed the door. As it opened, unknown things flashed past me as if escaping and I felt a certain amount of relief; I believe that by opening the door and facing my fear I released energy blocks such as fears and bad memories. I stepped forward into a black tunnel which led down to a dark and gloomy dungeon. (Remember, this was all going on inside my heart.) In the gloom I could see a number of large old boxes – again locked and closed. Warning me that I might find the contents upsetting, Raphael asked me if I was prepared to look into my past. Apparently these boxes held records of my past lives, and I was now being invited to view them. I felt apprehensive – it was cold and dark down in this deepest part of my heart and I couldn't imagine anything wonderful was going to appear.

I agreed to open the boxes and lifted the lid of the nearest one. I was immediately transported back to the 18th century somewhere in the Western hemisphere, either America or the Caribbean. I was present among a number of slave families and I was the slave driver, beating the slaves, killing some of them. As I looked on I shook with the horror of it and felt sickened with guilt. I knew what I was seeing was from my past and it was truly horrifying. But all the time the angels talked to me, counselled me, telling me that it was all right, not to feel guilty, not to be frightened, calming me. At the end of the scene a young big-eyed slave boy looked up and spoke to me from the past. 'Don't worry, Anne, we forgive you.' His sweetness and mercy went straight to my heart and I sobbed and sobbed – he was such an innocent child, without a touch of malice in him.

The angels explained how important it was for me to see my past and forgive myself. Otherwise, how could I be tolerant and all-loving to people in this lifetime who were going through similar situations, people whose characters and personalities I would otherwise not be able to tolerate? To be a good healer I had to love unconditionally, to be tolerant and forgive everyone. Before I could be completely unconditional with others I needed to be tolerant and forgive myself.

It was hard to come to terms with, but I could see their point. I knew that most of us have past lifetimes where we have been dark, even evil. These experiences are essential to our development as spiritual beings, for we need to have knowledge and touch all aspects of life and living, testing ourselves at the extremities of emotions and situations. I had been through a number of past-life regressions, where I had looked back through my past lives to help me understand myself, but in each one I had seen myself as a good person. I can see now that I had locked away the memories of my darkest time deep in my consciousness and covered it with shame.

As I forgave myself and let the past go, the dungeon and the dark tunnel disappeared and I stepped into a chamber lit by the most incredibly brilliant light – so bright it hurt my eyes. I knew I was in the presence of an amazing and powerful energy force. The angels stepped up and explained, 'This is the divine spark of love that is your true essence and the core of your being. This is what you were made from – you are created from the heart of God. You are seeing the energy of God, which is pure love. You are made of love. You are a creator made from the energy and essence of a creator.' Powerful stuff. Yet it has to be true, for we are all created from this essential source of love, and therefore that love is within all of us. I basked in this knowledge and let it act as a balm to my beaten-up emotions. After a while I stopped crying and thanked the angels and came out of the meditation. I had learnt so much, and had so much to absorb over the next few days.

An open heart flows with generosity

We continued our holiday, visiting spiritual retreats, ashrams, gurus and sacred places, but it was the time in the churches with the angels that changed my life. I had let go the past by forgiving myself. By removing those barricades of guilt I had faced and acknowledged my own sacredness; my own divine essence. Since that time I have seen deeper into the spiritual heart and understand the important role it plays in enabling us to be happy and live fulfilling and expansive lives. And I will share a process later in this book that will help you let down your own barricades and open your heart.

WHAT DID I LEARN?

Before we move on I would like to summarise the lessons I learnt from these amazing experiences and the effect that they had upon me.

✧ **Intention.** None of these experiences could have happened without my willing it and giving my permission. I believe it's through our intention to change that change happens. The angels explicitly asked me if I wanted to move forward. They also confirmed that it was OK for me to stay as I was. That truth applies to you too. You can stay as you are, that's fine. But if you want to evolve and change your circumstances and happiness levels, you have to make changes and allow changes to happen.

✧ **Letting down barriers.** We put barriers up around our hearts when we have been hurt and when we feel guilty. We do it because we believe this is the way to avoid the further pain that comes from having love then losing it.

An open heart lets in respect

However, you limit your experience of love and life if you keep these walls and blocks around your heart. I needed a push to bring my barriers down, but although I had a very loving life with no shortage of love I realise that with the barriers down my experience of love is richer and more expansive.

✧ **Forgiving and letting go the past.** When I forgave God I allowed myself to get close and feel the full impact of his/her love. If you don't believe in a proactive God then you may transfer those thoughts to the universe and the people you meet in your life. I realised that it was essential to love and forgive myself no matter what I had done – this allows me now to be forgiving and non-judgemental of others. Hate and bitterness, resentment and antagonism are barriers to our hearts. They stop love entering and, if they are severe enough, they stop us from loving. If you don't give love then you cannot receive love, so it's essential for you to clear the past by forgiving and letting go.

✧ **Compassion.** Through my experience with the small boy in Tibet I know that compassion opens our hearts. When we see someone suffering and feel a deep sympathy for that person we are experiencing compassion. Giving, whether time, money, or love and empathy for someone in need or pain, is compassion in action.

✧ **Appreciation.** I realised the meaning of the phrase 'use it or lose it'. How important it is to appreciate the blessings we have, whatever they are: good health, happy family life, prosperity, a good job, friendship, the beauty of nature. If we don't appreciate any aspect of our life for the blessing it is, then we will lose it.

An open heart lets in strength

✧ **Unconditionally loving oneself.** I have had this message so many times now. There are many ways to show that we love ourselves. Personally I must give myself the opportunity to relax, contemplate and enjoy quiet time. By balancing my life in this way I show respect for myself and my own needs. If we love ourselves unconditionally we can love others unconditionally and set the scene for fulfilling and loving relationships. No one is perfect, and as we accept our own 'imperfections' so we can accept them in our loved ones.

✧ **Our Divine Source.** When the way was clear I could see that the second chamber of my heart was filled with divine love. This was the most uplifting and awesome part of my inner journey – to understand that we all have the spark of God within. Our souls are created from a creator, so therefore we are of that same essence. I believe this second and hidden chamber is the Sacred Heart, which may explain why I had to have this experience and understanding in a Catholic church. I also realised that the divine is within us, not just above us. Whenever I meditate now I let my spiritual connection go through the chambers of my heart rather than up through the clouds. Once you draw up the blinds of your heart this inner light and love can shine out, and you then radiate love which will affect everyone you meet and all aspects of your life.

Since my heart opened I have gained an unimaginable inner peace. It's difficult to know what feelings and emotions other people experience. Many of us are naturally sensitive to the energy and emotions of the people we meet, and in my role of healer I open up and feel the energy of other people's

An open heart lets in compassion

emotions. But it's not easy to judge whether the feelings and emotional highs and lows are 'normal'. Often it's only when you have changed and let go that you realise there is a 'better' way to feel. I realise now that I always had a background noise of anxiety which was probably caused by my hidden guilt. Other people's emotional outbursts would send my stomach into a total spin. I can now identify the difference between my own emotions and what I am picking up from people around me. I am far more relaxed and less stressed.

My ability to channel healing energies has magnified, as predicted, and I believe this is due to my heart opening experience. When I am in healing mode I am a conduit for universal energies. Fears and guilt block this flow. As my fears and anxieties have diminished I have become stronger, bene-fiting my work and my private life. I've always loved angels but after their help on my journey I feel particularly close to them, more spiritually aware and connected.

I have also noticed that I wake up virtually every morning filled with a zest for life. Life is now a joyful experience rather than a struggle.

So, that's my story. I have written this book so that I can reach out and share with as many people as possible the insights and benefits that I now enjoy. I will share my under-standing of the spiritual heart and how to heal and open your heart, allowing you to receive the joys of love and the abundance of the universe. And without going anywhere near Tibet or India!

Are you ready for change? Do you want to move forward? If so, here we go – we'll start by looking more closely at what love really is.

An open heart lets in tolerance

THREE

What is Love?

This book is about love and how we can get more of it. So it makes good sense to start by looking more closely at what love really is, where we can find love and the differences between conditional love and unconditional love. There are different aspects of love that meet different needs in our lives and we will take a look at many of these now.

SOURCES OF LOVE

Most of us have a number of sources of love in our lives, some of which are apparent and some we need to seek out. You may be surprised, once you start looking for love, by just how many different types and hidden supplies of love there are available to you. We will begin with the people in your life and the love that may be on offer from them.

PEOPLE

Let's start with one of the most obvious and probably the most sought after – romantic love.

Love is tenderness

Love between partners – romantic and passionate

This is the love that everyone I know wants most of all. Virtually every single person I meet is constantly seeking the intimacy of a close and loving relationship, for there is nothing so wonderful as a romantic love when it works well. It can bring you alive and lift you to heady heights. At its best, it's not only loaded with the tenderness and support of togetherness but is fired by passion and sexual desire. It can set alight every fibre of your being, making you feel completely alive and vital.

If you ask most women, they will tell you that it's impossible to love more than one person in this close, passionate and romantic way. Some men may have a different view on this! However, most of us give our hearts to only one person at a time in this most intimate and passionate form of love.

Passionate love can be the most elusive love to find, for our expectations are high and the intimacy we have with a partner can in itself destroy this love. If you or your partner are too possessive and needy your emotions can become heavy and overwhelming. It is this form of love that requires the most 'work'. We need to be attentive to the quality of the love we are giving and receiving and constantly check that we are not letting it become tainted with controlling behaviour and manipulation. If you or your partner are emotionally wounded in any way, loaded down with baggage and issues from the past, your capacity to give and show love can be affected. It's therefore very important to heal the past so as to enable the full flow of love you expect from a close and satisfying relationship.

Because we give ourselves so completely to this love we are vulnerable to its loss and pain, so most heartache and heartbreak comes when it is lost. In Chapter 7 we will look

Love is caring

at ways of healing the pain of heartbreak and in Chapter 8 at ways to heal passionate and romantic relationships that have lost their way.

For this love to flourish you need to share, give and receive. So you need an open heart – a closed heart will prevent you from connecting in the first place. If your heart is closed many people you meet will sense the 'closed door' and walk by. Others may try to enter but may find the effort too difficult and move on. If you are having a problem finding a partner or keeping one, then you may well be 'suffering' from a closed heart. Stay with me – I will be showing you how to open that door!

Love between brothers and sisters – sharing, caring and supporting

This love grows in the intimacy of childhood, through the sharing and bonding that takes place when we play and grow together. If there is a big age difference between you and your siblings you may find that the bonding didn't quite happen and that you do not feel so close. Taking the trouble to remember birthdays, sharing time with your brothers and sisters and their families can open the door to a great source of fun and pleasure. Siblings generally have lower expectations and demands than partners, and this can be a light and uplifting form of love accompanied by the deep understanding that comes from living together through your formative years.

This love is well worth developing. My husband and his brother drew close after many years of distance when he brought a number of my husband's oldest school mates together to celebrate his fiftieth birthday. This was such a kind and imaginative gift that they became closer than ever before. We now make a point to have family days throughout

Love is a smile at a stranger

the year to bring us together, and these days are always filled with laughter. This love can be undemanding and fun, so make a point of taking time out to be together.

Love between friends – supporting, sympathetic and fun

This is an easy love to sustain, for we choose our own friends. However, if you are shy you may find it difficult to start friendships. If your heart is closed you may be sending out subliminal messages of rejection to people before they even have a chance to know you. People who have an open hearted and cheerful personality find it much easier to attract friends.

You may be thinking that it's not so easy to change your personality and that if you are shy and retiring it's painful for you to meet new people. However, as you work on opening up and letting go you will find that the causes for your shyness – low self-esteem, fear of rejection, and so on – will start to fade; and we will address these issues as we go through the book. If you find it easy to make friends, remember that keeping friendships vibrant needs work. Don't forget to pick up the phone – it's often friends that get left behind when romantic love comes on the scene, but it's the support and love of your friends that you need the most when passion is lost!

The majority of us can count the number of really close friends on one hand. These are the friends you would drop everything for, the ones you feel passionate about. You probably don't have time in your life to keep very close contact with many people, but by using the internet and phone it's easy to keep in touch just now and again with people with similar interests. Any close inter-reaction and connection with a person can lead to love. The closeness and warmth you feel even for those you don't see very often is a form of love and enriches your life.

Love within families – supportive, caring, binding and strong

This is another form of love that comes with high expectations. Parents expect their children will love them and give them a high priority in their life and children expect love and care from their parents. There is no doubt that love between parents and children can be the most supportive and deepest love and that the family can be the hub of your life. However, this love isn't necessarily there for everyone; maybe your parents are emotionally wounded and unable to love you or demonstrate their love, or maybe you have lost your parents already.

Losing – or never finding – the love of your parents can be a source of great pain and the reason for closing down your heart. However, if you allow this to happen you will be shutting yourself off from other sources of love. So if you are still waiting for approval, respect or love from parents who are unable to give it, please think again – make the choice to move on and find love elsewhere. But if relationships between you and your children or your parents are strained please don't give up, every now and again make the effort to show your love. One day you may be lucky enough to repair the damage and renew your relationships; in the meantime you can look for other sources of love.

Try not to dismiss any form of love. For example, the love that comes from step-parents or adoptive parents can be extraordinarily rewarding. Expectations are lower, but the intensity of the love can be just as profound if not deeper than that from natural parents.

Love is taking time out for another

Love between neighbours – respectful, sharing and tolerating

I cringe when I hear people making disparaging remarks about their neighbours and getting huffy about fences, borders, children and parking. There are a myriad reasons for distancing ourselves from our neighbours, for finding fault in their behaviour, but there is an abundance of support and love sitting there waiting to be enjoyed if you take the time and trouble. Not everyone is a good neighbour, I know, and some people are just plain awkward, but most people can be reasonable given the right approach.

It's easy to demonise someone you don't know – but once you have some contact with them they become real, and it's easier to be tolerant of someone you know. I have a friend who makes a community with her neighbours wherever she lives. The first thing she does in a new environment is ask the neighbours in for a drink and she has expanded her circle of friends this way. She has the added benefit of a long list of people she can ask to look after her plants and dog when she goes away!

The universe and God have a way of putting the people we need to meet across our paths. You may have a soul mate living in the house next door! But you will need to make the move to close the gap and get to know your neighbours better if you want to find the gem who might be sitting near you, just over the fence.

Love between people with a common cause – companionable and supportive

A great source of light and uplifting love is the camaraderie of shared interests and group activities. When we mix with people who have the same interests we magnify the energy of our enthusiasm. This aspect of love is very positive and invigorating. If we are creating something – whether it be pots, planes or a new charity – we become more productive when we are surrounded by others with the same intention. Joining a club or group can give you support and it is easier to break down barriers when you have a common platform of interest upon which to start conversations. If you join with an open heart you will get so much more from any activity, whether it be a club or a holiday tour.

Love between nations and cultures – respectful, tolerant and compassionate

Although you may think you cannot affect the love your country has for another, you can influence it by your own attitude and approach to different races, nationalities and creeds, either at home or when you are travelling. Tolerance and respect are forms of love and they are the basis for our chances of world peace. If you keep your heart open to other nationalities and cultures you are creating the environment for love between countries and nations to grow. There are organisations that focus on developing this love as a tool for peace, for example James Twyman's Peace Organisation. My own organisation, Hearts and Hands, has a Peace Initiative and offers distance healing. Both these organisations are accessible from the internet and you can connect to them in your own home.

Love between strangers in need – compassionate, empathetic and caring

Every time you smile at a stranger, help someone in need or give to a charitable cause you are giving out love. Hospices are a typical example of the power of love that strangers can offer. When a dear friend of mine died recently she was surrounded not only by the love of her friends but that of

Love is consideration and understanding

the carers and nurses in the hospice where she spent a beautiful and peaceful final week. As there is no expectation that we will receive love from the unknown people we pass in the street, the love they give us in times of crisis is extremely potent and can be profoundly moving. I become emotional just recalling the times I have needed help and received it from a stranger, like the driver who brought me down the mountain in Tibet.

All these are situations offering the opportunity for love to flourish. Some of them will feature in your life. Some may be more intense than others. And all of them, I am sure, can be stronger than they are, for we can never have too much love. I will repeat that because it is so very important and is the basis of this book – YOU CAN NEVER HAVE TOO MUCH LOVE! (I am shouting now!) No matter how many friends, how many family members, how many colleagues you have, you can always open your heart to another person both to receive and give love. As there is an infinite amount of love in the world, your capacity to give love is also limitless – you don't have to ration it or save it for a rainy day. This sharing of love does not mean that I endorse infidelity – I can sense your eyebrows rising. But it is possible to love more than one person in a generous, heart-open way.

It's not only people that can offer love. There are other sources that offer beautiful and powerful expressions of love.

ANIMALS – LOYAL, CONSTANT AND UNDE-MANDING

There is nothing more rewarding than the love of a pet. I am particularly fond of dogs and they are a constant source of love and affection to me. They don't mind if I have a bad

Love is helping someone through their difficult times

hair day – they forgive me for being grumpy or uncommunicative and ask for little in return for their loyalty and constant love.

I have a couple of friends who collect dogs. Although they will pass a newborn baby, they never fail to stop to pet a dog! They go dewy eyed when they talk about their 'babies' and are distraught when one is sick or passes on. The love they feel and are given in return goes deep into their hearts and satisfies a great need. They are both ardent campaigners for animal rights.

One woman I know has given up her banking career so that she can spend all her time rescuing and caring for animals in need. She has a collection of ponies, sheep, rabbits, dogs, cats and hens. You can feel her love for animals radiating from her, showing that this love is as valuable as any other and just as fulfilling.

NATURE – INSPIRING AND UPLIFTING

Do you find your mood changes when you walk through a forest or by the sea? Nature offers a form of love that can uplift spirits and make you calmer within, taking away the stresses of your daily life. It can nourish you and the more you appreciate it the more it offers. There are a number of ways to connect with this form of spiritual energy and love: gardening, rambling, surfing, climbing, star gazing, in fact any outdoor pursuit. When you connect to nature you are in touch with the spiritual aspect of yourself and life. God is within each one of us and also within every flower and tree. So when we appreciate nature we are appreciating God and opening energy pathways that simply overflow with love.

Love is sharing your money, possessions and time

DIFFERENT VIBRATIONS OF LOVE ENERGY

We have now looked at a variety of sources of love, but love energy can also vary in intensity, from unswerving devotion and adoration to mere liking. The energies of love come in different levels of vibration that can be experienced in various ways. Over and above the passionate and romantic love between lovers, there are many other ways in which humans can show positive feelings that can sustain them emotionally and spiritually.

◈ **Sympathy and empathy.** Sympathy is the emotion you feel when you see someone suffering and are concerned at their plight. It will usually spur you into action of some kind to help their situation. Empathy is when you actually sense, to a certain degree, the feeling of the other person – you get into their shoes as it were. These are powerful forms of love because they are positive vibrations and can be comforting to the receiver of the energy, replacing the isolation that often comes from suffering alone.

◈ **Compassion.** This is similar to sympathy but it goes deeper and opens the heart further. It can move you to tears, as shown by my experience in Tibet with the little boy with his burns. It is a beautiful emotion and comes through a sensitive heart. It is compassion that stirs us to give generously to charity. It is compassion that binds us to people we don't know on the far side of the world. The tsunami in 2004 opened people's hearts with compassion for the plight of those who lost their families and homes. I believe it will be love as compassion that will eradicate suffering in the world.

Love is taking time to stand in the shoes of another

❖ **Passion.** Passion is love with a touch of anger, with an intensity of feeling that makes action and creates change. When you feel passionate about a situation or a person you will move heaven and earth for them. Causes are started and brought into action by passion, for passionate love is a powerful force for change. Peace will come to this earth through passion – when we care enough to make the change.

❖ **Adoration.** This form of love can be one-sided. It implies a love that goes beyond unconditional. It is all-encompassing and absolute but it can be without discernment – loving without limit. When we love icons adoringly we rarely question and this kind of love can lead us down paths without caution. Although it's good to love unconditionally, it is wise to be discerning – otherwise we can be manipulated by the attachments of love. If you adore someone you are unlikely to ask about the motives for their behaviour and the consequences of your love.

❖ **Caring.** This loving is usually a practical form of love. Nurses care, community workers care, ambulance drivers care, doctors care. It's gentle and supportive.

❖ **Respect.** When we respect someone we accept them without judgement and hold them in some level of esteem. One can respect those who are wiser or have a better understanding than we have, like teachers, rulers, professionals (not all of them, of course!). When we respect another person's beliefs we accept those beliefs without necessarily following them ourselves. Respect for strangers and neighbours helps us to live together peacefully.

❖ **Tolerance and acceptance.** Tolerance and acceptance

Love is in infinite supply

are the emotional states that we are looking to achieve when we forgive. (We'll be looking at the force of forgiveness in Chapter 7.) It is difficult to show love to someone who has hurt you or someone you love, but by working on tolerance and acceptance you can at least create a sense of neutrality that will prevent harm. Living with tolerance will stop cultural wars.

Let's now look at the difference between conditional and unconditional love. Conditional love is love that comes with attachments and expectations. Unconditional love, in contrast, is love given totally freely, without constraint. Negative emotions that become attached to love, such as possessiveness or manipulation, can change its depth and quality. Expectations and demands set alongside the love can affect its value. No matter where love comes from – parents, friends, lovers or siblings, even our pets – it can be either conditional or unconditional.

CONDITIONAL LOVE

You may find that conditional love is far more prevalent in your life than you realised. Here are some examples of love that comes with a condition attached. This type of love does not come from a totally open heart – you can almost feel and sense the door opening and closing as this love is given out, based on your performance or what you can give back.

A lot of parental love comes with conditions:

✧ If you work hard at school I will love you.

✧ If you eat your dinner up I will love you.

Love and sex are both great but not the same thing at all

✦ If you visit me every Sunday I will love you.

✦ If you follow my instructions I will love you.

Romance and passion can also have a price:

✦ I will love someone who looks good.

✦ I will love someone if they have a lot of money.

✦ I will love someone if they love me.

✦ I will love you if you buy me presents.

✦ If you stay at home and look after the children I will love you.

✦ If you earn a lot of money I will love you.

✦ If you give me sex I will love you.

✦ I will love you if you are nice to me all the time.

✦ I will love you if you let me have my own way.

There can be conditions between nations:

✦ We will love this nation if it gives us its oil.

✦ We will love this nation if it thinks like us.

✦ We will love you if you have the same beliefs as us.

These are all circumstances of conditional love. It just doesn't work. It has too many strings attached:

✦ it's controlling

✦ it's possessive

Love is in the beauty of nature

✧ it's demeaning

✧ it's egotistical

✧ it's selfish

✧ it's manipulative

It's not love! It's purely a control mechanism put into words and flowered up to seem like love. Here are further examples of the way people give out 'love':

✧ the mother who showers her son with affection when he does well at school but reprimands and excludes him when he is struggling

✧ the nation that extends its arms of friendship and charity only to those countries that follow its own religious beliefs

✧ the man who is critical of his girlfriend and buys her gifts when she does what he wants in bed but hits out when she isn't interested

✧ the spiritual leader who loves only his flock and is intolerant towards non-believers

✧ the couple whose love flies out the front door when financial difficulties arise

✧ the woman who is only affectionate to her husband when he is agreeing to her wishes

✧ the person who loves their friendly neighbours and dislikes the ones who keep themselves to themselves

As you read these examples of conditional love you will see that they are embedded in the behaviour of many people

Love is in great music

you know – you may even recognise that you pull some of these strings yourself! Don't feel guilty – most love in the world is given with conditions so that we become part of the pattern without realising it. But once you understand and can FEEL the difference you will want to change. Then the love you give will begin to be unconditional.

UNCONDITIONAL LOVE

The love you are looking for is love without any conditions at all. A complete acceptance of everyone you meet, warts and all. And being completely accepted yourself by others and, very importantly, by yourself. This is the love that will open your heart. This is the love that will give you total fulfilment. This is the love that will change the world.

✧ Unconditional love will heal the wounds between nations, between families, between partners, between friends, between strangers.

✧ Unconditional love offers forgiveness as second nature.

✧ Unconditional love is love that pours straight from the heart without the mind putting its oar in and discussing the pros and cons.

✧ Unconditional love is total acceptance and total toler-ance.

✧ Unconditional love looks for the positive in someone rather than finding fault.

✧ Unconditional love flows from heart to heart without interference from thought and logic.

Love is in the eyes of a baby

The main aspects of unconditional love are tolerance, forgiveness and total acceptance. This means that you need to see past the human frailties, the irritating habits and quirky characteristics of your partner, friends, neighbours or work colleagues. It is far better to focus on their good points and learn to overlook their weaknesses. Gossiping and making negative comments about a person will only aggravate the situation, for your thoughts and words are a negative energy that will drive a wedge between you. It will also have a detrimental effect on the person you are talking about – even thinking about – because your thoughts and words are energy that goes to the point of your focus and will seriously affect the energy of the person in your mind.

You have probably experienced walking into a room and knowing that people are talking about you. It can affect the way you feel. Thinking negatively about people, whether it's your sister-in-law or the next door neighbour, is a habit and like all habits it needs work to change. Try to catch yourself every time you think badly of someone – even if you are only pointing out their obvious faults. Later we will be talking more of the power of forgiveness to heal our hearts. However, forgiveness also helps to open the channels of love between everyone in our lives.

If you think you love someone conditionally, ask yourself why. It may just be that they have a different way of looking at things, different tastes, different lifestyle choices, different cultural approaches to life. Maybe they have different expectations of life from yourself. This is particularly noticeable in family situations where children have different outlooks and expectations from their parents. We are all profoundly affected by the way we are brought up, the experiences of our childhood, the mood and nature of the country and government and by our own soul's sensitivity. All these things affect the

Love is magnanimous and all forgiving

way we behave and treat people around us. So it's highly unlikely that our children will have the same tastes and needs as we have, as they have been brought up in entirely different situations from ourselves. With tolerance you can love them for what they are and not for what you want them to be.

Living with unconditional love can become a way of life, it's a habit that you can develop. But it takes working at! We will now look at some guidelines that can help you work towards a goal of filling your life with unconditional love.

Love is a helping hand

FOUR

How to Love Unconditionally

Turning your conditional love into unconditional love will not be easy. There will be many challenges, there will be times when you must remember you are not a saint as your human side comes to the fore; your patience will be tested and your ability to tolerate stretched to its limits. Family members need special care because even the slightest sign of annoyance can be taken to heart and held on to for years. This chapter contains action plans, visualisations and techniques which will help you to reprogramme your outlook and approach to loving those nearest and dearest to you.

Starting a journal at this point would be a good idea. Keep a notepad with you and by your bed so that it's available for any work you want to do. As you work your way through this book you can keep a note of any insights, ideas or thoughts you may have on the love or lack of love in your life.

With true love you are set free

HOW DO YOU LOVE?

Before you start to change, let's see what your current attitude is to those nearest to you. Do you in fact love them conditionally, or unconditionally? Or perhaps you may even have a negative attitude towards them. Here are some questions to help set you thinking about your feelings and attitudes towards those around you and who share your life and time.

✧ Do you love your neighbour? Would you drop everything to go to his or her help?

✧ Do you love your mother and father? Would you visit them just because you know they love to see you?

✧ Do you love your children even when they are noisy, dirty and disobedient?

✧ Do you keep an open heart to everyone, no matter how distasteful they are to you? How about that loud-mouth in the next office?

✧ Does your partner show you respect at all times?

✧ Does she or he love you when you scratch the car? Ah, that's a good test!

✧ How possessive are you of the people around you? How would you react if your family decided to go away for Christmas without you?

✧ Do you grit your teeth when certain people call you?

This will have got you started – now list everyone you know and make a note of how you love them.

With true love you are open to create

YOUR INTENTION OF LOVING UNCONDITIONALLY

Having considered how you feel about the people in your life, you may have found that you are conditional with some of your loving. You may also discover that you don't actually like some of the people in your life! That's OK, for you won't like everyone in your family or your workplace. You certainly won't like everyone you meet! You are bound to prefer to be with some people rather than others. However, it's one thing to find someone irritating, another to build up a negative attitude towards them.

How can you start becoming unconditional? Well, first of all *you have to want to.* All change in the way you are and the way you live your life begins with an intention and a commitment. You need to make that commitment strongly; as strongly as you made the commitment to bring more love into your life. Here are two ways to reinforce your commitment to learning to love unconditionally.

◇ **Write it in your journal.** The very act of writing it down will reinforce the energy. As you write the force of your emotions and thoughts go into the paper.

◇ **Say it out loud** as though you are taking an oath. Your words and the sounds you make are energy, and words spoken positively and with determination have a high frequency. This high vibration energy will stay around you, giving you strength and reinforcing your will. It will also flow out to the universe, and the universe – or all that is, the greater consciousness of all – will respond to every commitment, vow and intention. From the moment you declare your intention to be more positive in your

With true love you become strong

way of loving those close to you, you will find that it gets easier and easier to be tolerant and loving. The most brilliant part of this intention and change of approach is that as you love more and give more *you will receive more!* The universe and everyone around you will respond to your positive energy and as you give out more love so it will return to you.

LOVE IN ACTION – SHOWING UNCONDITIONAL LOVE

You now need to follow up on your intention with action in order to reprogramme yourself to love unconditionally. Here are some ways that you can put into action your intentions of giving out unconditional love and positive vibes:

◇ **Make a habit to forgive rather than hold grudges.** When you think back to a past upset or trauma you actually reignite the negative experience and refuel the bad feelings that you had when it occurred. By letting go the past you can release the negative emotions that associate with it. This will make it easier to love. We will be looking at a powerful process of letting go in Chapter 7.

◇ **Shrug off criticism that comes your way rather than take umbrage.** See yourself as too big to worry about the little jibes and barbs that come your way. Duck them. Don't allow them to stick. It's your choice – you can take them to heart and find fault with yourself and the person who is sending them out to you or you can imagine them passing through you and beyond you. It's a wonderful feeling when you can just smile at the person

With true love you flourish

who is attacking you. Try it out. It's a great way to strengthen the energy of love, for it helps take you out of the state of fear and into a positive state of peace and calm. This is great preparation for opening your heart.

✧ **Always look for someone's good points and try to ignore their bad ones.** It's empowering to play to your strengths and ignore your weaknesses. In this instance, try playing to the strengths of those around you. Praise their good work and let go their bad. Your kind words and positive comments about their achievements are words of unconditional love. This is love in action. You will have an immediate return of love when you work this way. Gloss over the inadequacies of your partner, child, work colleague, friend or parent and major on their good habits, attitudes and acts and you will see them changing their attitude and approach to you too. I believe we can all benefit from looking at our strengths rather than our weaknesses and it may help you to form more positive attitudes if you focus on good points, on the strengths of the people you mix with, rather than their weaknesses. This is also a habit that can change your perception of people and you will be surprised at some nuggets of gold that lie beneath the exterior surface of many you will encounter. Scratch a little and you may find aspects of their character that make it easier to love and accept them.

All of us tend to react badly to criticism – becoming vengeful and fighting back. But if you keep reminding people of how good they are, they respond positively and lovingly. They also become empowered, and when people are in their strength they normally act more benignly than when they feel threat-ened. Of course, if you are an employer there may be times

With true love you become your own person

when you need to point out an incorrect practice, but you can always do this in a humane and caring way.

⬧ **Take a 'live and let live' approach to neighbours and work colleagues.** You may come across someone who you just cannot like. If you find someone intolerable, irritating or upsetting then avoid them where possible. If you are sharing your life or work space with people who think differently or act differently from you, just let them be. Act as a role model and you may be surprised how people will copy your own positive and loving way of being. Just let go those who don't harmonise with you. Take your lunch breaks with someone who thinks like you, smile and walk by those who irritate you. Don't antagonise your next door neighbour, who is upsetting you with their behaviour, but shut them out of your mind.

⬧ **Give help and care whenever you can.** Whenever you get the opportunity to show love in any caring way, just do it. Don't worry about how someone will react. So many good intentions and thoughts go no further than the mind because people are worried how they will be received. Just do it. You will regret the things you don't do far more than the ones you do.

⬧ **Use distant healing.** By sending out love to others in the form of prayers or distant healing, you will be speeding up your heart opening. You don't need to be a qualified healer to do this and neither do you need to know the person to be effective. Simply put your hand on their name or picture and hold the intention of sending a stream of love from your heart to them. Send it without condition – be happy for them to use the love in any

With true love you grow to your greatest potential

way they wish, whether it be to heal physically or emotionally, to release stress or to become more energised. If you wish to do this on a regular basis you can join my organisation Hearts and Hands as a distant healer – see the end of the book for details.

✧ **Be positive about everything, including the weather!** Positive thoughts are high vibration energy and they send out an aura of light and love around you. This radiation of love will also attract the energy of love. Every negative thought and word lowers the vibration and when your energy is low and depressed, your low vibration will attract negativity. So see your glass as half full and not half empty, say positive things about yourself and others, keep working on seeing the good in people, situations and circumstances. Gradually it will become a habit. Write in your journal all the positive things that you can think of about yourself, your life, your friends, your work, your home, your country, etc. Acknowledge that there will be weak spots, faults, etc., but for this exercise just think of all the positive points.

✧ **Be good to yourself.** Self-love is essential if you want to love others, so treat yourself well, give yourself time, do the things you enjoy, surround yourself with loving friends, avoid saying negative things about yourself. Remember that you are a spiritual being on a journey through life – for this journey you have taken a body and personality, but you are still essentially spiritual. Recognise that this means you are essentially created from love. Focus on your strengths and good points and allow yourself to make mistakes without beating yourself up for them.

With true love you can reach for the sky

These are some ideas of how to give yourself opportunities to bring positive loving actions and thoughts into your life – and don't forget, the more love you give out the more love you get back. Keep reminding yourself to give your love without strings, without conditions and without attachments. Let's now see how we can reinforce this love by putting it into action to show the people in your life how you feel about them.

COMMUNICATING LOVE

If you have a shy or introverted personality you may find it difficult to take your feelings and put them into action. However, it's no use sitting at home and thinking loving thoughts about people without showing or indicating in some way what you feel. It's only through the interaction of kindness and other aspects of love that you will start to receive love. You are the starting point. Love comes from you and will return to you but you have to be the initiator. So how can you share and show your love? Remember we are working towards your heart opening. Loving acts, loving words and loving intentions are all keys to opening the door.

Some people find it really difficult to show the love they feel. I had a mother-in-law who was like this. She loved her son but whenever he visited her she would spend the entire time nagging him and putting him down. He knew she loved him but boy, it would have been helpful if she had shown it more often. She would buy him gifts and I think she thought that was enough. I am sure she thought that actions speak louder than words and that her gifts were proof enough of her love.

Sometimes actions are a great measure of love, but it didn't

With true love you can express your feelings

quite wash with me that she held her son's best interest at heart, especially when she could be quite shrewish in her comments about him. Harsh words go deeply into our psyche and create wounds that can take years and years to heal. I often meet people whose angst and problems go way back into their childhood, caused by careless, thoughtless, hurtful words from someone they loved.

Children normally continue to love their parents and hold them in respect no matter how they are treated. The effects of the painful putdowns and detrimental comments do not necessarily show up till much later. I have had people say to me things like 'My father didn't love me as he would beat me if my school reports were poor.' I am sure the father did love the boy and was desperate for his son to do well at school. However, beating someone or shouting at them for their lack of achievement will more often block them with fear, diminishing any chances of fulfilling their greatest potential rather than spurring them on to success. Any form of abuse, putdown or negative attitude can leave a mark. However, every act of kindness, concern or care will instead leave a warm memory that will help build strong and loving relationships.

As an energy healer I feel the energies of my clients. When we release the negative energies of putdowns such as 'You're no good', 'I don't know why I had you', 'You're useless', and so on, I feel a stream of dark and heavy energy leaving the person. You may have a child or a partner who presses your buttons, irritates you or rubs you up the wrong way, but do take care with your words. Loving words on the other hand uplift both you and the person receiving them. There is nothing, but nothing in the world that a child or adult wants to hear more than 'I love you.'

Simple signs of loving can send out the signals of uncon-

With true love everything is possible

ditional love. Make a point to do one or more of these acts of gentleness and tenderness to show your love to your partner, friend, brother or sister, mother or father:

✧ Touch their arm when you are speaking to them.

✧ Put your arms around them and give them a hug. Make it a big one, totally enveloping the other person, hold them with your hands outstretched touching their back.

✧ Kiss your friends hallo when you meet. The French do this with everyone they know. What a great way to start a meeting!

✧ When meeting and greeting a stranger, shake and clasp their hands with both your hands – it makes your welcome that much more friendly.

✧ Rub the shoulder of your dear one next time you pass them.

No one to hug? Then give yourself a great big hug – that will do very nicely, for loving yourself is the starting point of healing yourself completely!

Breaking family patterns

You may have been blessed with loving parents who shared and showed their feelings. However, not every child is so fortunate. Many children come from broken or dysfunctional marriages and don't get to see positive bonding, so they have to learn it for themselves as they become adults.

If you were one of those children, make a decision to break the family habit and start a new way – give your parents signs of your affection, give your brothers and sisters

With true love you can feel at ease with yourself

a hug when you see them. I can tell you that after the initial surprise they will respond; remember that everyone wants love. Before long you will find them doing the same. I've tried it with my extended family and it always works. Make a point of giving your own children plenty of affection. Even when you are tired or depressed yourself it will make a huge difference in their lives, and this will reflect back to you too.

SAY IT – 'I LOVE YOU'!

If you love someone, why not tell them? We have a family habit of ending every telephone conversation with 'I love you'. I think it's a great way to say goodbye. My parents were brilliant at showing their love, so I was brought up with positive demonstrations of love around me. We kissed each other on meeting and leaving, while they frequently held hands and were spontaneously generous with their hugs. It was therefore easy for me to be demonstrative, but everyone can adopt this habit. It's just the best way of sending out the vibes of love.

If you have a culture that discourages public demonstrations of affection you can certainly show tenderness to each other at home. This will send great messages out to your children and be excellent role-modelling for them in their future relationships.

DO IT NOW

Your life can be ruined by regret. If there is someone in your life whom you love, tell them and tell them now. Put down this book, make a phone call, send an email, write a card – tell someone you love them. It's a great feeling when

With true love you can share everything

you see the smile these simple words bring. You can never do it enough, for I don't know anyone who complains about being told they are loved! If it feels a bit sloppy – a bit uncool – then use the words that suit your group or culture; just ensure you get the message across.

The day before my father died I rang him three times. I normally phoned my parents daily but that day I kept getting the urge to connect with them. I spoke at length with my father and as usual we shared our sentiments and said how much we loved each other. He died of an unexpected heart attack the next day and I had a heartbreaking journey from the north of England down to my parents' home in the south. Naturally I was full of grief, for I loved him dearly, but I didn't have to face the regret that I hadn't told him how much I loved him. This was a blessing and it helped his passing. Guilt and regret can eat away at you and spoil your inner peace for years. It can also block your ability to receive love or give love to others.

Pam

A dear friend of mine, Pam, died recently after a painful illness. Her daughter, although obviously devastated at her mother's passing, was very happy that she had been with her when she died. She spent the hours before Pam passed on holding her hand, talking to her, telling her how much she loved her, thanking her for the love she had given and encouraging her to pass over. She felt there was a completion that may not have been so profound if she had not had the time or the inclination to share her thoughts and love with her mum before Pam went.

You may be sitting there now worried about words or actions in your past. There may be someone to whom you could have said the I LOVE YOU words but didn't because

With true love you can be honest

of your own inhibitions or their difficult personality – maybe they have passed on by now, while you are left with regrets. However, it's never too late.

IT'S NEVER TOO LATE TO SHOW LOVE

If you feel that you missed the chance to tell someone who has passed on that you loved them, please don't be anxious, for you can do this now in a meditation. In a meditative state we move our spiritual essence closer to the astral planes where the spirits of those who have passed on reside. This allows us to have a meeting point halfway between the dense world of our living reality and the light and etheric world of spirit. Here is a guided visualisation that will lead you to meet your loved one in the spiritual and heavenly planes.

Meditation to show love to someone in spirit

◈ Find a quiet place and allow yourself to relax; sit in a comfy chair or lie down on the floor. Avoid a bed, as you are likely to fall asleep!

◈ Drop your shoulders and breathe in deeply for a few moments. Gradually feel your body becoming softer and more fluid.

◈ See yourself as a great tree and see your roots growing deep into the ground beneath you. Feel the connection with Mother Earth and allow her nurturing love energy to come up through your legs like sap rising.

◈ Now imagine that you are walking through woods on a

With true love you can overcome obstacles

sunny day with the breeze rustling the trees around you. Ahead you see a gate that leads into a closed, walled garden. This is your healing garden. Approach the gate, open it and enter the garden.

✧ Here you will see the garden of your dreams filled with your favourite flowers. Walk through the healing environment of this serene and tranquil sanctuary. After a while you will come across a bench beside a waterfall. Take a seat on the bench and relax, listening and watching the falling cascades.

✧ You will become aware that someone is moving towards you, stepping out of the watery mist of the falls. You recognise the person and stand to welcome them.

✧ Tell them everything that you have waited so long to say – tell them of your love and if you wish give them a cuddle or hug. They will respond, for they can feel your love and understand your intention even if you cannot visualise them clearly. Allow yourself to unburden your feelings and express your love in any way that suits you.

✧ Finally, sitting side by side, spend some time enjoying the closeness and feelings of love that flow between you.

✧ When you are ready, say farewell – know that you can meet up again in this magical garden. Leave now and close the gate behind you. Walk back through the woods into your room.

Well done – you should now feel lighter and released. Bless you.

With true love you are set free

LOVING STRANGERS

It's relatively easy to show your feelings to those close to you but it's also important to radiate out your love to strangers. In your quest to get more love into your life you need to keep sending it out. Let's see how we can share love with the people we meet but don't know intimately.

To communicate your feelings during chance encounters and with strangers who cross your path, you can share your appreciation of any service or kindness by speaking up at the time or you can write letters, send emails or telephone. If someone has done something that has helped you, whether it be a waiter in a restaurant, a cabbie, a worker in a call centre, a bus conductor, a shop assistant – make it a practice to thank them profusely and smile as you do it. If the help has been outstanding write a letter. This is unconditional love in action.

As you make it your daily practice to smile and show appreciation to everyone, you will begin to naturally radiate love. As you send out a flow of love the law of karma (what you give out will come back) – the boomerang law – goes into action. Love will start to flow straight back to you. Don't leave any of this to tomorrow but step out now and start the change. Start right now.

AT WORK

In the workplace you won't necessarily want to go up and give your boss a big smacking kiss every morning – well, then again you might! But you can give out praise to those around you. Encouragement and praise are great ways to show positive feelings and will create a good atmosphere around you too. Try to leave your ego at home and allow others to shine

With true love you are open to create

around you – I know it's not always easy in a competitive work situation, but if you are sure of yourself and have confidence in your own abilities you will be able to be big hearted with colleagues and give them credit where it's due. All these are aspects of heart opening and giving unconditional love.

Action:

✧ Tell someone in your workplace how good they are at their job.

✧ Tell someone how much you appreciate what they do for you.

✧ Next time you go to the supermarket, give the checkout assistant a big smile and a thank you.

✧ Ring someone, email them or write and tell them how much you love them.

GIVING LOVE ATTRACTS LOVE

As I mentioned before, the wonderful and amazing fact about loving is that the more you give out the more you get back. And you don't get the same amount of love back – no, you actually get more! However, and this is a big but – you may not necessarily get it back from the focus of your love. For example, you may love your mother and spend hours looking after her and caring for her. She on the other hand may be incapable of giving you love back and you may well feel distraught about this. However, the very act of loving will open your heart and as long as you are receptive you will find that love will come back to you from others, magnified a thousand times.

With true love you become strong

It's a natural law of the universe that what you give out will come back. It's the yin and yang of life; the reaping what you sow. It's quite amazing how this works and I have seen it time and time again. Unfortunately, if, as in my example, you were focused solely on your mother and expected to get love from her, you would very likely be disappointed. This might lead to resentment and even self-pity. Remember to keep your antennae on the alert, for love can come from unexpected quarters. It can also come in surprising ways – in a manner you may not expect. For example, it can come as kindness from a stranger when you are in need, or as an unexpected gift.

I am fortunate in my work that I connect with strangers all the time. I often get letters from readers who have found my books helpful and I can feel the love that comes from them in the form of gratitude. But you don't have to be a healer to find that form of love. My friend Brenda has a natural ability to open up and communicate with anyone she meets and she has turned this skill to helping all sorts of people. In Malaysia, where we lived together for some time, she was a regular visitor to the local Cheshire Homes where she sat and chatted to the inmates, learning their entire life stories and becoming friends to all of them. They loved her. She has a knack of making people feel relaxed. She now visits a local care home and spends time with the residents listening to their stories, their problems and their life histories. She gives out love and makes people feel good about themselves, and so she is loved by them in return.

By giving, you receive. Love doesn't normally come knocking on the door so you need to take a step or two out to receive it. When you help the old lady down the road you open the energies to receive. You are giving out love when you visit a friend in hospital, take in their

With true love you flourish

washing, feed the neighbour's cat and so on. When the energy of love goes out it will attract love back in. A small kindness can open the way to a stream of love from unexpected places.

Action:

✧ Write down the names of all those people outside of your family and friends who have shown you special care in your life. Think of doctors, nurses, neighbours, workmates and so on. How did they make you feel about yourself? Remember the kindness of their actions and words.

✧ Think of your family and friends now and, forgetting any hurt they may have caused you, focus on the love that they have shown. Write down any particular loving act that had an effect on you.

✧ Then write a list of the people *you* have loved – passionately, caringly, compassionately, any way of loving. What did loving them do for you?

Before we leave this chapter on how to love unconditionally, let's take a look at the way children love. They love unconditionally and they do it naturally. We all have a small child within us, so let's take a few moments now to connect to this natural and simple approach to love.

TAKING A CHILD'S PERSPECTIVE OF LOVE

Children have the knack of getting right to the point. They see through the illusion and fabrication that we use to

With true love you become your own person

confuse and complicate our lives. They have a terrific approach to love. They can give love in an innocent and undemanding way. They manifest a positive aspect of love – unconditional love without prejudice or judgement. Children have a simplistic view of life generally and through their eyes we can see a different world; a world where the good is very good and the bad hurts. They are naïve and innocent and therefore not judging. They do not dismiss you and with-hold their love if you are having a bad day, have lost your job or your self-esteem, put on weight – they love you for who you are and they love without reserve.

I once received an email which demonstrates this simple approach to love. A number of children were asked 'What does love mean?' I am not sure of the source and its validity but the answers are quite delightful and thought-provoking anyway! I have given some of them throughout the pages of this book so that you can share this pure and simple unconditional love through their eyes.

I also asked my friend Debbie to put the question to her little girl Kaia, aged five. Love, she answered, is 'When two people give each other kisses and hugs and it feels soft right in the middle of your heart.'

Debbie asked her, 'And where is that?'

Kaia responded by placing her hand on the middle of her chest and said, 'It just feels like love.' Bless her, she's learnt more in her five years than a lot of people I know have learnt in a lifetime. Well done, Kaia!

What's your definition of love? Maybe you would like to ask the younger members of your own family and those of your friends – it could be an eye opener!

Within each one of us there is still a child who wants to love, be loved, have fun and be recognised. As we grow and life takes us forward we let go our childish ways, but now

With true love you grow to your greatest potential

and again it is good to reconnect to the child inside and to allow it to have fun, to let go the inhibitions that limit our life. Small children don't fear rejection as adults do; small children don't see the bad things in their parents, only the good; small children see actions and words as the pure manifestation of feelings. To reconnect to the sweet and simple approach to love, let's get in touch with our inner child and let it come out to play.

Meditation to reconnect to the innocent love of a child

In this exercise you will be going back in time. To help you to recall your childhood view of love, you can use this symbol for clarity by drawing it in the air before you start your meditation.

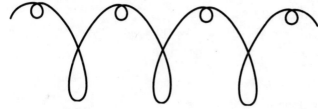

Clarity Symbol

Draw this symbol in the air from left to right and repeat three times. It will bring back memories with a greater clarity.

✧ Close your eyes and relax. Feel your feet making strong connection with the ground. Breathe in deeply and slowly four times.

✧ Visualise yourself walking through woods towards a walled garden. You reach the garden gate, set into high walls. Open the gate, step inside and close the gate behind you.

With true love you can reach for the sky

✧ You are in a safe and tranquil garden, filled with your favourite flowers. Take a few moments to enjoy the serenity and peace, for this is a healing garden.

✧ Now you will see a line on the ground – this is a time line and as you walk along it you will be taken back in time. Know that you are going back to your earliest childhood days. Walk there now. Allow yourself to be the child that you were.

✧ Call in a time when you felt great love for your mother, father, sister, brother, grandparent or pet. Allow yourself to feel that love, sense the sweetness of that love. Enjoy this time and discover further times of great joy from your childhood, acknowledging the feelings of innocence.

✧ When you have finished, bring that same sense and feeling back into your life and world again now, as you walk back along the path into the room.

Well done.

You are already on your journey to discover more love and open your heart. We've looked at what love is, we've discovered that unconditional love is what we need, we've considered the sources and the importance of showing love. We will continue to focus on how you can personally start the process of bringing more love into your life. In the next chapters we will look at the reasons why you are closed to love and find ways to heal the emotional wounds and heartbreaks that may have caused you to shut the door to receiving the love you want and need.

With true love you can express your feelings

FIVE

Heartache and Heartbreak

In this chapter we look at the reason why so many of us have our hearts closed. We look at the issues that wound our hearts – how betrayal, abandonment, death of a loved one, emotional and physical abuse can cause such pain that our spiritual and emotional heart centre becomes damaged, resulting in heartache or heartbreak. We will look at the way severe heart wounds can create problems in the way you face life or react to life experiences and even leave you with long-lasting effects such as emotional instability.

Bear with me if you are feeling impatient to start your repair work, for we need to delve into the causes and acknowledge the source of your problems before I can take you through the healing process. Once you have established why and how your heart has become damaged, you can then open your heart and heal the wounds.

First let's look at how the scars created by heartbreak and lack of love affect us and the way we change to compensate.

'Big hearted' - an open heart filled with love

OUR NEED FOR LOVE

Most heartache and heartbreak come from the loss or lack of love. Why does love affect us so drastically? We all have a deep desire for love and we need it for our wellbeing just as we need food and water. However, when we have been hurt we close our hearts, put up blocks to receiving love and change our behaviour and perspective on life. We even look in other directions for substitutes for love. All of these reactions take us further and further away from the love we crave and need.

LOVE ENERGY

Your body is a form of energy and each individual resonates on a different vibration and wavelength. In the same way, every emotion has a different energy frequency. The emotions of fear, hate, bitterness, anger are negative and have low, heavy frequencies. They lower your spirits and deplete your life force energy. The emotion of love has a high frequency and will uplift and raise your life energy, so you feel good when you are loved, loving and in the presence of love.

Love energy is also a powerful force for healing. In my healing sessions I channel the universal energies of love and pass them to my client. As they open to receive this love their energies lift above the negative states of disease, troubled mind and emotional imbalance and turmoil. Love actually transforms negativity. Every physical cell requires love, so when you are sick you absolutely crave it. If your heart is closed then you will not be able to receive the love you need to flourish physically and emotionally. You have an energy centre that plays a vital role in the process of receiving and transforming the action of love.

'Heart strings' - cords that connect loving hearts

THE HEART CENTRE

The hub of all the activity of love, the energy of love and the emotions of love – both giving and receiving – is your heart centre. So let's take a closer look, not at the physical heart but the 'heart' that gets broken when we lose love.

Your heart centre is a force of spiralling energy located more or less in the centre of your chest. The position can vary but it is where you feel the pain of heartache or the fullness of great happiness. This is one of several energy centres known as *chakras* (Sanskrit for spinning wheel) which pass energy to all parts of your body, interlinking your emotional, mental and physical energy bodies. Your heart chakra affects and reflects your ability to receive and give love. As all aspects of your system are connected, any emotional suffering through loss of love or heartache can affect you physically. Therefore, when you open and heal your heart centre you positively affect your physical state.

When you connect to the spiritual aspect of your heart centre it may help to visualise it as a chamber that holds your personal source of love; within it see a flame sending out a clear light that holds the same vibration as love. Love uplifts your energy levels and your spirits, bringing positive thoughts and feelings of wellbeing. When you fall in love, for example, you experience feelings of joy and ecstasy, you become light and uplifted. And when you receive and give love your energy centre spins in a spiral of pure light. If you could see this as psychics can, you would see it radiating pink light. Green and pink are the colours associated with the heart centre, green being the vibration of the heart centre and pink the vibration of love. Roses hold this same love vibration, which is why we associate pink roses with romance and love. For years my spirit guides have shown me pink

'Heart sore' – suffering the pain of lost love

roses in meditation as a sign that they are happy with what I am doing. Since pink roses turn up in my life wherever I go, I have chosen the pink rose as my logo.

HEART STRINGS

The thoughts you have about a person you love create a stream of energy, an etheric cord, that links your heart to theirs; heart strings that connect you and join you in love. These too are pink! Energetically and spiritually these cords link and bind you and are the source of great support and happiness. They can flow between friends, family members and partners, even to those that you admire and hold in high esteem. For worship of any kind, including celebrity worship, will create a cord. You may remember the outpouring of grief when Princess Diana died. Many people around the world had admired her and held her in high esteem, many had loved her image and what she stood for. They had created cords between themselves and her as an icon, and when she died they felt the loss as their cords dissolved.

For you to be physically and mentally stable, healthy and balanced, you need love to flow through your heart centre continuously, for if you are deprived of love your spirit will wither and fail. One reason your heart may fail to flow with love is if it has been wounded.

HEART CHAKRA WOUNDS

The pain of a traumatised energy heart centre can be as intense as physical injury. When you lose someone you love, the pain you feel in your chest is the pain of chakra tearing. This is the source of the expression 'heartbroken', for your heart centre can be ripped apart by great loss as the love

'Heart break' - the pain in your heart centre when love goes

cord is pulled out – literally by its roots – and the source of love removed. This happens when someone you love dies or a lover leaves you. If the loss is sudden the pain can be extreme and severe.

Time will heal the tear and the emotional trauma and you should be able to re-establish your self-esteem, recover from the pain and find someone new. However, if you are unable to 'get over' the loss it may be that you are still attached by your cord and continue to yearn for the person you have lost. This lasting attachment can prevent you from opening to new love, for your heart will still be attached to your previous lover. In Chapter 7 we will look at ways to detach your cord and heal your heart so that you can again receive love, for you will only be open to love if you have let go and healed the past.

IMPRINTS

Imprints are the images of experiences that are burnt into your etheric energy body and soul, which is the part of you that comes back time and time again in different physical forms each lifetime. These wounds hold the memory of the pain, shame and trauma deep within you at cellular level. You may recall the trauma that caused the imprint, or it may be from an unknown source from childhood and lie deep in your subconscious. It can even come from a past life. Whenever you face a situation similar to the one that caused the initial wound the pain can start. It may manifest fear, a loss of confidence, a background anxiety that you live with continuously, or low self-esteem. In fact many outcomes and effects can be brought about by these scars.

Love uplifts the spirit and opens the mind

Peter

Past imprints and scars associated with love can affect your ability to give and receive love now. Peter lost his wife, Suzie, when they were in their twenties. She died suddenly and tragically from a stroke that left her in a coma and Peter eventually gave permission for her life support to be turned off. Her death broke his heart. The pain was so intense that this created an emotional wound that imprinted his consciousness. The pain went so deep and the trauma so intense that the imprint took years to release. It was just like a scar with the pain awakening when he started to get emotionally involved with another woman and for eight years he was unable to make a close relationship. Whenever he started to feel emotionally involved he backed away as he was filled with fear – fear that this woman too will eventually leave him. The imprint of Suzie's death had left him fearful of love as he associated love with pain and grief. Initially he didn't understand what was happening and just thought he couldn't find someone that he wanted to share love with but eventually he understood why he couldn't find love, he realised that by closing his heart he was shutting out love, he was excluding his chance of happiness. He spent time healing the past and consciously letting the door on the past close without feeling guilty of shutting off from Suzie. He has now met a lovely woman who with sensitivity has helped him to overcome his fears of involvement and he is now very much in love.

Love nourishes mind, body and soul

WHAT CAN WOUND YOUR HEART?

We'll now look at some of the experiences that are the major causes of heartache, heartbreak and heart wounding. Knowing the cause of your problems can help you understand why you react in certain ways to situations and people and your entire healing process can gain momentum. I will start with one that most of us have experienced at some time in our life.

REJECTION

Rejection and the deliberate removal of love can affect you profoundly. It can be particularly painful to be rejected by a parent. A child of a split marriage will often feel abandoned by the parent who leaves home. Children often think they are the cause of trouble between their parents, so they too can feel guilty.

Marie

Marie felt that she could no longer stay in her relationship and decided to move out. She could not afford a home big enough for her two girls, aged 12 and 14, and to avoid them further disruption suggested they stayed with their father in the family home where she would visit them every day and cook their meals. She constantly told them she loved them and would continue to stay close, but her move severely affected the eldest girl. After a year Marie and her husband reunited; they reconstructed their marriage and worked at healing their own wounds. Unfortunately, the eldest girl couldn't adjust. She experienced mood swings and bouts of uncontrollable anger and aggression, most of which she directed at her mother. These emotional symptoms came

Love heals anxiety and fear

from the scar or imprint that her mother leaving left within her, affecting her heart centre through the withdrawal of love and the soul with the fear of abandonment.

With counselling it became clear that she felt let down and rejected by her mother at the time when she needed her most – as she was moving from childhood to woman-hood. She has now healed most of her wounds and thankfully her relationship with her mother is recovering, but it has taken an enormous amount of work from both of them and a long and traumatic adjustment process. The imprint of being left behind and abandoned by her mother will still be deep within her and could come to the surface again with any close relationship she makes. She may well have in-security issues with anyone that she gets close to.

There are many forms of abandonment and rejection. Some are more extreme than others and we all react differently depending on our personal character and vulnerability. The example of boarding schools comes to mind. Some children thrive on the community living, while others are emotion-ally wounded by the separation from their parents. Many of the adults I know who were sent to boarding schools early on – from the age of six – have the symptoms of abandoned children.

PARENTS' DIVORCE

I mentioned that some children feel rejected when their parents divorce, but that is not the only wound caused by divorce. The splitting up of a family can leave imprints that create insecurity and anxiety within other relationships. Experiencing a beloved parent leaving can break your heart, and the scar of this can lead to mistrust and insecurity, and

Love heals the past and gives hope for the future

in later life to a reluctance to commit to a relationship for fear that it will not last. If you have seen your parents fall in and out of love several times then you too may have difficulty in sustaining a long-lasting and rewarding relationship. If your parents argued and were mentally or verbally abusive you may find you behave in the same way, or you may become unable to cope with any form of discord or disharmony. If one parent used force to dominate, then you may be unable to express your feelings or share your opinions, fostering low self-esteem.

Difficulty finding love – June

June is a very attractive and vivacious young woman and yet has a real problem finding and sustaining a loving relationship. Her problem is insecurity and this goes back to her childhood and the problems she experienced with her parents. She was brought up by step-parents and wrangling parents. She was well loved but the constant arguments between all those responsible for her parenting left her anxious and insecure. She falls in love quickly and throws herself at men. This can be disconcerting for a guy who wants to feel that he has done some of the chasing. And the love she offers is smothering and overpowering – men feel threatened and withdraw fast into their caves, or disappear. She is then heartbroken and her insecurity grows. Her insecurity and low self-esteem make her too keen to please, and she subjugates her own personality and needs so that men can't get to know who she really is.

Difficulty with long-term relationships – Mary

Mary is an older woman who has had problems all her life with long-term relationships. Her mother left and went overseas when she was eight and she was brought up by a

Love dissolves prejudice

stepmother who was less than gentle. She is extraordinarily attractive and men fly to her side, but every relationship flounders. She is strongly independent and her partners feel inadequate, as if they aren't really needed. Her childhood experiences made her self-sufficient and she needs to be totally in control of her life. She is charming and kind but she is reluctant to let go her controls, and this makes it difficult for her to allow a man completely into her heart and life.

So divorce or acrimonious parents can leave deep scars for children. As we grow, these scars can affect our ability to give and receive love or form stable, loving relationships. Were you affected by the way your parents got along together?

LOSS OF A LOVED ONE

Any loss can cause you grief, the loss of anyone or thing that you are attached to – loved ones, pets, homes, friendship, work. The wounds of losing a loved one can stay with you for a very long time.

James

James is still affected by the loss of his mother, who died in his teens. It left him angry and hurt and the wound was intensified when his father remarried soon after. He found it almost impossible to accept his stepmother and resented her terribly. It's only in his forties that he has opened up to her, but the wounds have left him closed down. He has difficulty in really enjoying life and shrouds everything with pessimism, fearing the worst will come from every situation.

Love brings the colour to your world

Etheric cords

As well as creating etheric cord attachments to people, we can be connected by etheric cords to places and situations. If you are employed for a long time by one company or love your work, you can become closely attached. When my husband retired he suffered all the symptoms of grief. His heart was broken, because he loved his work and it was a huge part of his life; it was his identity and his passion. So when he left he felt the loss as strongly as if he had lost a living friend, one he had shared every day with.

A client of mine came to see me a short time after her husband's death. She was not only suffering from the loss of her loved one, which broke her heart leaving her with severe heartache, but because she had been his carer through his illness, she also felt the loss of her role. The struggle to reclaim her life and happiness left her depressed and lacking in energy. She tried to heal her depression and her inner void with alcohol, which was giving her further challenges. As she heals her heart and comes to terms with her loss she is now managing to regain her energy and get back to work. Her work is giving her life a purpose and making her feel needed again.

Links to the past – Gill

When a person dies their soul travels back to the astral planes of the spirit world, the gardens of heaven, our spiritual home. It's important for those left behind to let the spirit go by naturally grieving, then moving on with life. If we cling too strongly to their memory, yearn endlessly, perhaps even create a shrine of their room, we will prevent both the departed and ourselves from moving on spiritually. These debilitating attachments can be reinforced by strong emotional ties of anger, love and guilt.

Love is a feeling of belonging

Gill is a healer. Her son died of cancer a couple of years ago, but she found it difficult to grieve and in a form of denial she continued her work. Eventually she too developed cancer. After ignoring its existence for some time she eventually had treatment, and only then accepted healing from her friends. Eventually she began crying in the course of a healing session and the dam burst. The release of her tears helped her enormously. She confessed that she had held back her grief because she felt guilty that she had not saved his life – she had been unable to heal him.

Parents often feel responsible for the death of their children, as they hold a natural responsibility for their welfare and happiness. We cannot influence when a soul leaves this earth, for that decision is for the soul alone to make. As Gill realised and acknowledged this she let go her guilt, released her emotions and opened herself to receive love again. She then began to heal.

In Chapter 7 we will look at a powerful process that will help you to let go any cords holding you attached to people, places, jobs or countries – in fact anything where the attachment is causing you heartache.

Allow the tears

I can't emphasise enough the importance of grieving and releasing emotions. In some countries it is customary for mourners to hammer their chests in public and wail out their pain. In the West we are very reluctant to show any signs of emotion in public. However, it will speed up your healing if you let out your grief, either by writing down your feelings or talking them over with a friend or loved one.

Love is a deep understanding of each other

The rollercoaster

The loss of a loved one is typically followed by shock, then denial, then self-doubt, leading to depression, then adaptation, before final acceptance. From my experience the first year of loss is the worst and these twelve months can be extremely painful. Of course, you will never forget the person who has gone and you will be affected on and off for the rest of your life. But the very severe pain and the sense that you will never recover should start to leave you after the first year.

The Rollercoaster of Change

The loss of anyone or anything that you love will leave a scar. Do you still mourn the loss of someone dear to you?

FEELING UNLOVED

Sometimes we can be loved without seeing it, understanding it or acknowledging it. If you perceive that you are not loved

'Big hearted' - an open heart filled with love

it can have the same effect on your heart as if you were really not loved. With this perception you can harden your heart towards a mother, father or child who you think has given you less love than other family members. If you see situations from only your side without standing back and understanding the bigger picture, you can easily fall into the role of victim.

Andrew

Andrew, the son of a friend of mine, is convinced his father favours his sister. This has hurt a lot. He has developed a chip on his shoulder and he sees himself as a victim. He doesn't believe anything good can happen for him. Men often treat their sons differently from their daughters and are less soft and tender towards them. In Andrew's case he has misread the situation. Actually my friend loves his son very much and never hesitates to support and help him where and when he can. But still Andrew holds the view that his father doesn't love him and it affects all his relationships.

Your emotions are affected not by what happens to you but by the way you perceive and respond to the experience. If you *think* that you have been cheated, betrayed or treated unfairly you will *feel* the consequential emotions and their effects. Your perception that you have not received love, or have had it withdrawn from you, will cause heartache as intense as you would feel if you were actually not loved.

A sense of betrayal – Simon

A sense of betrayal can hurt your heart and create a barrier. Simon, a 44-year-old businessman, received bad news regarding his grandmother's will. She had decided to leave the boys out of her will, leaving all her money to the girls

'Heart strings' - cords that connect loving hearts

in the family. He is devastated. Not only was he banking on the money to relieve his finances but this is the second time this has happened to him. His father remarried and left all his money to his second wife when he died, so his inheritance will only come to him when she dies. Simon sees this as a sign of rejection, a denial of love. He is devastated and feels betrayed and unloved. Unless he moves on from this pain he will be sadly affected for some time.

Do you feel that someone, or even life generally, has been unfair to you? It is essential to heal these suppressed feelings and bottled-up emotions, for they will severely handicap your chances of inner peace and happiness and will affect the level of love you can receive. Bitterness is a barrier to love and to happiness. Resentment is a poison that can fester inside you.

ABUSE – EMOTIONAL AND PHYSICAL

The worst impact on your heart is any form of abuse, particularly when it's from someone you love. I frequently see the results of abuse in my healing room. I've felt and sensed the deep pain and scars. If you are in an abusive relationship at the moment, I hope that this book will help you to heal the damage of the past and give you the strength to create a future free from this damaging behaviour that batters not only your body but your self-esteem.

Some men and women go from one abusive relationship to another as though they are unable to attract loving and supportive partners. Some tell me it's a feeling that they don't deserve love. Others say that any relationship is better than being alone and are thankful for any signs of love; some mistake the possessiveness of a domineering and overbearing lover for true love. If you have never received love as a child

'Heart sore' - suffering the pain of lost love

then it is difficult to distinguish the real from the fake. Bullies will manipulate by giving sex, gifts and attention, and will do this all in the name of love. They will become obsessive and jealous, a sure sign that they too have a problem with love and may have been abused or neglected in their own childhood. The jealousy that comes from paranoid posses- siveness can often lead to physical or mental abuse. It can be frightening and often dangerous.

This problem is not just one that affects women. Men can be mentally, emotionally and physically abused by women. If a man has been completely dominated by his mother as a child, then it is possible that he will seek the comfort zone of a strong and dominating partner. If he has never been able to stand up to his mother's abuse, he will be easily intim- idated as an adult and may repeatedly slip into similar relationships.

The pattern of abuse

Even mildly abusive relationships can form a pattern and I have known people who enter them repeatedly. Years ago I had a friend who moved from the north of England to work in London to escape her husband because he beat her. She was a bright and outspoken young woman and seemed full of confidence and life. After a year she started dating one of our work colleagues, a lovely man, and eventually married him. All her friends were delighted for her.

After a year I went to visit them and I couldn't believe the way this 'lovely' man was treating her. He shouted at her and talked down to her and humiliated her in front of her friends. And worse still, she let him! It would seem that she had changed this man in some way – maybe she drew out the worst in him. She definitely seemed to be forming a pattern of difficult marriages.

'Heart break' - the pain in your heart centre when love goes

Making the change – Suzannah

I have known people to go from one abusive relationship to another, but I have also known women who have made a stand and decided that this was not what they wanted in their lives, and have subsequently chosen a very different partner. It is great to hear stories of the worm turning!

Suzannah has two young girls and was married to a very dominating and emotionally abusive man. He found fault with everything she did, humiliated her and frequently told her she was stupid. She believed him and began to lose her self-respect and confidence. She felt incapable of living a normal life, she became housebound and too nervous to make social contacts.

When he began complaining that she was fat, she finally responded. She took courage, joined a gym and booked a personal trainer. Her trainer spent hours with her, not only helping her improve her physical wellbeing but also rebuilding her self-esteem. She gained confidence through the work she was doing in the gym; she took her trainer's encouraging words to heart and began to feel stronger and more at ease with herself.

One day her husband pounced on her when she took two biscuits to eat. 'Look at you, you're fat, you're stupid, you're ugly,' he started his usual ranting. 'No I'm not,' she replied coolly. 'I don't care and I'm leaving you.' And she did – all because of two biscuits! Good for her. I had a lovely letter recently telling me that she had never felt better and her confidence was growing day by day. She is happy with who she is and at peace now, even though she has the challenge of bringing up her children single handed.

Does your life follow a pattern? Do you consistently attract abusive partners? Do you have any negative patterns you would like to break?

Love uplifts the spirit and opens the mind

Sexual abuse

Rape and sexual abuse can result in fear of the opposite sex and quite understandably, a revulsion for sex. This is a terrible shame, as sex with love is one of life's greatest experiences. Professional counselling is advisable if you have suffered either rape or sexual abuse, but you may find that the exercises and process that I will lead you through in Chapter 7 will be beneficial and help you to let go the demons of the past.

Jean

Jean, a young woman I have known for several years, has battled to release the effects of being sexually abused by her father. It badly affected her self-esteem and she has worked for years in order to build up her self-confidence and accept herself and what happened.

The pain she suffered emotionally spilled into her physical body by way of the holistic osmosis that interrelates all aspects of our being. Whatever pain we suffer, whether physical, mental or emotional, will permeate throughout our entire being. She held her pain in her lower back and hips to the point where walking was extremely painful for her. The pain she suffered emotionally spilled into her physical body through the holistic osmosis that interrelates all aspects of our being; whatever pain we suffer whether physical, mental or emotional will permeate throughout our entire being. As she healed and forgave her father and loved herself, the pain diminished. She has also been helped by a very loving and sensitive husband who has supported her through her healing.

Judy

Judy, another client of mine, has battled with her weight all her life after she was abused by her brother when she was small. She said that she felt guilty and dirty and she believes she put on the weight to create a barrier and to stop herself from being attractive to men. She too has healed the wounds and has come to terms with what happened. She has found peace and is happy in a loving relationship and is delighted that after many years of trying unsuccessfully to lose weight, she has now managed to shed her 'padding' and found a svelte, slim figure underneath!

So it is possible to heal even the very darkest and most painful abuse and find happiness and a loving partner. Needless to say, I sincerely advise anyone who is living with someone, either male or female, who is physically abusive and dangerous to move away and find refuge. I know it's hard – any love can seem to be better than no love – but true love is a tender and supportive emotion, not a hard and cruel one. In Chapter 7 we look at some practical steps you can take.

FEELING LET DOWN BY GOD

If you see God as all-powerful, all-controlling and all-loving, then there may well be times when you feel that he has let you down. Why doesn't God help me? If God is so powerful why doesn't he get me that job I need? Why doesn't God cure my illness? Why is he not answering my prayers?

This reaction to God and spirit is quite normal and many people have an issue with trust and faith – quite understandably, when you see the suffering that exists in the world. However, this is another barrier to pull down, for God is the source of the greatest and purest love and if you are closed to this you are missing the greatest joy of life. As I found out in my own experience, you create your own barriers between yourself and God.

Love heals anxiety and fear

GUILT

We now come to one of the greatest blocks of all – guilt. If bitterness is a barrier, guilt is a portcullis, an impenetrable cold block that shutters off the deepest recesses of your heart. It is sneaky, for it can lie dormant for a while. Just when you think you can relax and enjoy yourself, it comes back with its icy grip around your heart; your stomach sinks and you remember. You feel helpless because you cannot change the past but you are still attached to it. Sometimes guilt is connected to someone who has died – leaving just the regrets. If only I had treated him better, if only I had told him I loved him, and so on.

Jennifer

I shall never forget the intensity of Jennifer's self-loathing, caused by guilt at her unkind treatment of her grandmother, who had recently died. She lived in a tiny flat in Hong Kong with her mother, father and grandmother. Whenever grandmother spoke, Jennifer would jump down her throat. Yet she really loved the old lady and after she was gone Jennifer had sleepless nights worrying about her behaviour. The guilt niggled constantly like a toothache. We worked on it together, and I used the power of loving healing energy to heal the scars of guilt. She then allowed herself to forgive her past behaviour and come to terms with her relationship with her gran. If you are suffering from your past actions, don't despair, for emotions can be healed. You may not be able to change the past but you can change the way you feel about it. If you have trouble letting go of these imprints yourself, you may consider visiting a healer. The love that a healer gives you can have a remarkable effect on the scars and imprints of heartache and guilt.

Love heals the past and gives hope for the future

IMPRINTS FROM PAST LIVES

I believe our soul makes many visits to Earth, each journey giving you an opportunity to develop and grow. You have a divine blueprint that is your long-term mission and in between each lifetime you make a plan for the life ahead. During these life cycles on Earth you experience many things – some that uplift you and bring you joy and some that cause you pain.

Many imprints are healed there and then through forgiveness and spiritual growth. Some, however, stay with you when you re-enter the Earth plane, waiting to torment you again. This explains why you may have issues that you bring in with you, inexplicable fears and anxieties, a sense of being drawn to some people as though on spiritual elastic, a sense of déjà vu when visiting certain places; why you may recoil from certain situations, or experience difficulties achieving financial security or creating fulfilling relationships.

Fear from the past – Claire

I have been helping Claire, whose family were at best dysfunctional and at worst abusive. Both her parents were heavy drinkers and her father died when she was ten years old. After her father's death she had nightmares that her family would become destitute and that she would be given away. There had been no indications that this would happen but her father's death was a trigger. From that moment she suffered doubts and insecurities, and her life has been a constant struggle.

During her healing sessions I saw a couple of her past lives. In one her parents had just died and she was a bedraggled little thing in a poke bonnet being dragged off to a workhouse – I felt terrible sadness and she had an awful

Love dissolves prejudice

life. Another life flash was of a young woman dying alone in poverty. In her healing session we released these memories of the past and the associated fears that had made her so insecure in this lifetime.

CONSEQUENCES OF HEART WOUNDS AND IMPRINTS

We have now looked at just some of the scars and imprints you may have collected and which have caused your heartache and heartbreak. These act as barriers to your spiritual heart centre. This means you may be shutting out love even when it is coming towards you. It means that you may be avoiding opportunities to be loved. It means that you may reject and spurn love. Sometimes you won't even see the love that's there for you. You may be sending out energies like silent messages, saying that you don't want a close relationship. You may also be sending out unseen energy messages that attract abusive love, possessive love or even no love at all. I want to remind you that with intention, determination, time and some help you will be able to heal, no matter what has happened to you. We will take a short look at some of the consequences of heart wounds before we start the opening and healing process.

At the beginning of this book I identified the results and situations you may be facing if you have a closed and wounded heart and not enough love coming into your life. Let's again look at the possible outcomes of the scars of love and how they may affect your behaviour and response to people and situations. The possible consequences include:

✧ doubting your ability to cope on your own

Love brings the colour to your world

✧ being involved in constant quarrels and altercations

✧ fear that others will not accept you as you are

✧ being unable to cope with emotional situations

✧ the feeling that people are out to get you

✧ lack of self-respect – blaming yourself for everything

✧ difficulty in seeing the roses, let alone smelling them

✧ struggling to make partnerships work

✧ a feeling that life is a battle

✧ a constant feeling of anger deep within you

✧ a constant feeling of anxiety

✧ feeling misunderstood

✧ difficulty in keeping a loving partner

✧ a feeling that your parents didn't love you or want you

✧ inability to either attract financial security or to hold it

✧ attracting abusive relationships

✧ attracting unsuitable lovers – those that are married already or living far away

✧ saying yes when you mean no

✧ giving to others but being unable to give to yourself

✧ never taking time to rest, relax or do nothing

✧ feeling obliged to put others first

✧ being obsessed with thoughts of someone who has gone

Love is a feeling of belonging

These can be roughly grouped into the following basic feelings and attitudes:

✧ lack of self-esteem from lack of self-love

✧ the feeling of being a victim – self-pity

✧ bitterness

✧ fear

✧ the feeling of loss of control or direction in life

✧ the feeling that something is lacking

✧ grief

REACTIONS TO HEARTACHE, HEART-BREAK AND LACK OF LOVE

As we have seen, the many different causes of heartbreak leave scars and imprints, and these will show themselves in your behaviour and attitude to life. Here are some of the ways people react to the pain of heartbreak.

USING SEX

It's easy to mix up the need for sex with the need for love. It's been a joke for a long time that women give sex to get love and men give love to get sex! When a woman starts to jump into bed indiscriminately there is usually a pain deep inside that she is trying to heal. She is looking for love to heal either low self-esteem or just generally fulfill a lack of love in her life. She may misguidedly think that sex will

Love is a deep understanding of each other

bring love along with it. When a man jumps into bed indiscriminately he is driven by testosterone and probably just has a high sex drive!

Reactions can be even more intense for sex abuse victims, where a father has manipulated his daughter and made her think that what he was doing was an act of love. Such experiences will leave a mixed-up feeling about love, resulting in either complete rejection and fear of sex or an overwhelming desire to sleep with anybody and everybody in a search for the happiness that is supposed to come from love and sex.

ANGER AND RESENTMENT – MAGGIE

Emotional pain of any kind can cause deep resentment, bitterness and incipient anger. Maggie is a young woman in her twenties who recently completed her teacher training. However, she found when she started her work experience that she could not relate to children – in fact she didn't enjoy being with them at all. This sudden loss of direction brought on a huge panic attack and she was overcome with waves of emotion and anger. All the frustrations and fears that she had held on to since childhood came pouring out.

Her father and mother had both been alcoholic and she had been brought up with the fear of knowing that any time Dad would start hitting Mum again. She learnt to be good and unobtrusive. She learnt to shut down her feelings and closed her heart. As a result she has never had a close relationship and the 'boxes' that hold her old emotions are cracking open now. Anger about stolen childhood, particularly directed to an abusive father and a passive mother, is quite normal and I see it as a step towards healing. Once Maggie's emotions are healed and her heart is open she will be able to experience open relationships again without fear.

'Big hearted' - an open heart filled with love

CLOSING DOWN

Emotional pain will make you shut down to some extent. If you close down your feelings too much you may find it hard to relate to someone you love. I have a friend whose husband is unable to feel anything. He loves his wife but he can't describe the feelings. This goes back to his younger days with a dominant and frightening father and a strict schooling. He learnt to hide and suppress his feelings when he was young. Now he can't cry and he can't feel the joy of his wife's love or his own.

One of my friends had a boyfriend who was born in Africa and was sent off to boarding school at the age of six. He remembers carrying his teddy under his arm and crying night after night until he was bullied so much by the other boys and the matron that he stopped. He hasn't been able to cry since. Their relationship was spoilt by his inability to connect and express his feelings and eventually they split up.

DEPRESSION

The ultimate shutdown is the state of depression, where you fall into a deep pit, feeling sorry for yourself, losing direction and interest in life. Prescription drugs can help a little but they don't resolve the cause and don't heal the wounds. If you find it hard to get up in the morning, are always tired and listless, can't be bothered to get involved with things, see every task as a mountain, then you could be suffering from depression to a greater or lesser degree. And this could be the result of some loss or deep hurt. Depression is difficult for the sufferer and their family and friends. Healing and love can help. I have seen people transformed once they have learned to accept love and let go the old dark energies.

'Heart strings' - cords that connect loving hearts

FINDING FAULT WITH YOURSELF AND OTHERS – INTOLERANCE

Do you constantly strive for perfection? Do you find fault in everything you do? Do you find fault in your body? Intolerance is a sign of lack of love. Often the problem is lack of self-love and we will look at healing this later. Lack of patience and never being satisfied are also signs.

Pat, a young friend of mine, recently took her exams and when she heard that she had ten As and one B she cried for a week – not for joy, but because she was disappointed with herself for not getting all As! Her expectations and goals are set at an impossible level. She is a perfectionist and the root cause is her lack of self-acceptance. Once she heals her heart and opens it fully and loves herself more, then she will be happy with her achievements. She will always strive to do well, but hopefully she will judge herself less harshly.

SELF-ABUSE – CUTTING, EATING DISORDERS

Self-abuse is a desperate effort to mask emotional pain that cannot be relieved or healed in any other way. Fifty per cent of those practising self-mutilation have suffered sexual or physical abuse which has left deep scars of low self-worth, anger and heart wounds. The physical pain of self-mutilation is easier to bear than the emotional pain. Unable to express feelings and fearful of relationships, the self-abuser will use cutting to release and express frustration, anger, pain and inner turmoil. Eating disorders such as anorexia and bulimia are also signs of lack of self-love. You may be surrounded by loved ones who cherish you, but if you are wounded you will not be able to see and appreciate their love.

'Heart sore' - suffering the pain of lost love

USING DRUGS, ALCOHOL, OVEREATING

Some people will turn to alcohol or drugs to dull their inner pain and distress. Of course, these only offer short-term results, leaving you with feelings of self-disgust afterwards which only exacerbate the situation. I have helped several alcoholics in my time as a healer and they go through a terrible spiral of self-loathing and guilt. Drugs, alcohol or food are used to bring inner peace and contentment, to relieve the inner torment. But the fix is short term, then the spiral starts again – this time overlaid with guilt. Once you reach the peace and inner calm that comes with total healing, then the need for these short-term remedies and quick fixes goes away.

Having identified some of the consequences of heartbreak and heart wounds, we can now move on and discover how to open the door to your heart and allow in love.

'Heart break' - the pain in your heart centre when love goes

SIX

Opening Your Heart

In this chapter we will look more closely at the spiritual heart, the heart centre, and I will share the insights I have been given by my spirit guides about the way love affects us, body and soul. I will then guide you through a heart-opening process similar to the one I experienced in Tibet and India.

THE SPIRITUAL HEART

During my journey with the angels in India they introduced me to a new way of seeing myself and my heart centre. I will now describe to you the various chambers or dimensions of the heart. I will describe these chambers as I saw them, but don't worry if you see them in another way – allow yourself to go through the experience without worrying about the detail. Just let your own imagination give you the sense and vision that works for you. But whether you see dimensions, rooms, temples or levels, you will find yourself going through a series of doorways.

As you use this information later, in your own meditations,

Our hearts are open when we respect each other

you may find that you go through the doors in a different sequence from the one I use — don't worry about that. Some doors may be closed and others open, depending on your own personal experience and situation — just remember that this is your own personal journey. I, however, always go through them in this order when I am meditating, and so I will guide you through them in this sequence.

First I will introduce the chambers to you. If you find as you read that you start to experience a feeling in your chest, it's a sign that you are already starting the process of opening — so just go with it and allow it to happen! To prepare you for this connection with your spiritual heart, and to help you let go of your mind, logic and physicality, we will start with a short visualisation.

Visualisation to release the physical and connect to spirit

✧ Close your eyes and breathe in deeply four times. Drop your shoulders and relax.

✧ Imagine that you are surrounded by a bubble of pink light. Feel your body getting lighter and lighter as the energy of the pink bubble fills you.

✧ Tell yourself that you are now connecting to your spiritual body. Give your attention and focus to your heart centre, in the centre of your chest.

✧ Visualise a flight of steps leading down from your mind to your heart centre. See yourself walking down these steps and getting smaller and smaller.

Our hearts are open when we accept each other

> ✧ You are now standing in front of a door. Know that this is the door to your heart. You are now connected and spiritually aware of your heart centre.

I will now lead you through the chambers – you can just absorb this description for now as an introductory tour.

THE FIRST CHAMBER – PERSONAL LOVE

The door opens to the first chamber, which is the source of your personal love. There is a candle flame burning in the centre of the chamber that represents the love that you give to others. This chamber is the source of the love you give to your family, friends, colleagues, pets, the people you meet who touch your compassion, the world, religious and spiritual masters, gurus, etc. Any love that you give out to the world and offer to others and yourself is sourced from this flame, from this chamber.

This door should not be hard to open, but you may find it so if you have been so badly hurt that you find it hard to give out love. If that is the case, you need to work on giving love; love meaning respect, care, tenderness, acknowledgement, understanding – whatever is your interpretation of love. Try to love as unconditionally as you possibly can. Notice the colour and feel of this chamber – ideally it will become light and pink as you heal and develop your capacity to love. Remember it is in your nature to love. As this door opens and you hold the intention of loving, so the love will naturally start to flow.

Our hearts are open when we communicate honestly

This first chamber is filled with the energy of the people you have 'taken to your heart'. In meditation you may see them, and you will be surprised how many have taken up residence – it's a great place to be – in your heart. Anyone you have loved will be attached by an etheric cord to this chamber, giving you a constant source of their love too. When someone we love leaves us and breaks or pulls away their cord, it is this chamber that hurts, it is this heart that experiences the pain of rejection or loss.

The angels showed and explained to me something that many of us don't realise; that this source of love is available for ourselves as well. To be open to the infinite love of the universe, of the world and the joys of living a limitless and expansive life, we need to be loving and caring of self. We will look at this more closely in Chapter 8, as it's an essential aspect of your loving and healing.

THE SECOND CHAMBER – THE SACRED HEART OF DIVINE LOVE

This chamber is entered from a door at the back of the first chamber. It is the chamber that holds the divine spark – your own source of divine love, the God that is within you and the essence of God that is who you are. This is your true identity as a spiritual being. Knowing that you are created from the source of love is a fundamental truth that allows you to be as big as you can be and grow to your greatest potential in life. While this door is locked you can never really come to terms with who you are and love yourself entirely. This is the door that is barred by guilt and the deep pain caused by the damage of lost or withdrawn love.

This door is locked if you have rejected God as creator

Our hearts are open when we laugh with each other

and source of love. I believe we are all God and this divine heart energy of love is God. So every thought and every emotion is part of God, everything that is created is of God and is God. The Heart of God is the source that creates the vibration of energy that is your soul. It's not easy to explain this God within and God the creator as separate beings, for the energy is the same and the energy is love. I think you can swap the word God for Love anytime. Therefore, as you are God you only need to acknowledge this to open the door. You only need to realise that all that matters is love; to love yourself so much that you open the door and let go the guilt and separateness that keeps you apart from this amazing inner source of divine love. It's this love that has the power to create and to attract the life that you so desire. So if you are to grow and achieve inner peace and happiness, opening this door is really, really important.

You can open to inner peace and happiness without going through meditations and complex spiritual processes. Anyone who is completely at ease with who they are, who loves life to its fullest and sees the best in all, has opened that door within. If you are in any way unhappy with your life or feel discord within, then this door needs a hearty shove! It is this door that is the key to opening your heart. Remember you are opening your heart to receive. Once this door is open you will be able to receive all the love you want.

If you have problems opening this door you need to focus on releasing guilt, loving yourself, allowing yourself to be joyful and allowing yourself to enjoy life. In the next chapter we will look at many ways to heal. But holding your intention to accept your divinity, accept that you are forgiven, accept that you deserve love and joy will take you a long way down the path of healing this beautiful heart chamber and reconnecting you to your divinity.

Our hearts are open when we are patient with each other

THE THIRD CHAMBER – THE CHAMBER OF THE UNIVERSAL HEART

Beyond the chamber of the Sacred Heart is another door. Through this doorway you can connect with everything in the world, every tree, every rock and every human. This dimension of the heart opens you to the feeling of oneness and connection with all. The same energies flow through all of us and all of us are created from the same source. Not only humans but animals, insects, birds, the vegetable kingdom and the mineral kingdom. You can connect with anything and allow its energy – its love essence – to come towards you. You can absorb this energy and use it to give you the powers and strengths that you need.

Here are some examples of ways that objects and people can give you universal energies of love. You just need to be in your universal heart and focus, in other words just think of them:

✧ A **mountain** gives out energies to inspire when we feel demotivated, to strengthen when we feel weak, to give solidness and connection to the Earth when we feel insecure.

✧ A **stream** can send clarity when we feel muddle headed or unsure.

✧ A **tree** gives security and shelter. Sensing the roots entering the earth can give stability and grounding when you feel spacy and unfocused.

✧ A small **child** connects us to motherly love, bringing out the strength to cope, as well as innocence and purity.

Our hearts are open when we understand each other

✧ A **herd of animals** can give the energy of companionship when you feel lonely.

✧ **Crystals** offer the energies of healing.

✧ A **lion** represents courage when you feel daunted.

✧ The **moon** represents the feminine energies of love – nurturing and gentle.

✧ The **sun** gives out strong and powerful masculine energies, but is also life-supporting and uplifting.

✧ **Venus** sends forth the wonderful energy of romantic love.

✧ A **valley** and a nestling cottage offer shelter when you feel vulnerable.

✧ **Falling water**, rain or a waterfall is cleansing and clearing – allowing you to purify your thoughts or your body.

✧ **Fire** gives you passion and strength.

✧ A **rose** gives you the energy of perfection and completeness when you are striving towards finishing a task.

Action: Write a list of all the energy streams that you would like to absorb and the objects that represent them to you. When you do your meditation later you can call these in to give you the values, strengths and energies that you need.

Every race and culture gives out energies of different vibrations. You can also gain human strengths and inspirations by connecting to role models, people who you admire and respect.

Our hearts are open when they sing with love

Here are some of the people, some living, some in spirit, to whom I connect when I need their energies for inspiration:

✧ Mahatma Gandhi – for passive determination

✧ the Dalai Lama – for compassion and forgiveness

✧ Nelson Mandela – for greatness and forgiveness

✧ Jesus – for unconditional love

✧ Archangel Michael – for protection

✧ Kwan Yin – for guidance and love

✧ My mother – for love and encouragement

You can make your own selection of those that inspire you.

The energy of the universal heart state is powerful and uplifting; feel yourself growing huge and sense that everything and anything is possible. Feel all limitations falling away and all the obstacles that come in your way just dissolving. It's a truly powerful place because there you can connect to everything good about the world and people. You can tap into the force of the human spirit at its most magnificent, connect to the fine and loving thoughts of everyday people – which is the force that will take us on to a better and more loving world. I believe that life will get better and more loving; there will be a time when there are no more wars, no more disharmony and discord between people, races and nations. I believe that when the wounded souls and damaged hearts are healed we will 'ascend' into another way of living that is more peaceful and more loving, joyful beyond our greatest dreams.

Our hearts are open when we solve problems together

THE FOURTH CHAMBER – THE CHAMBER OF ANGELS AND SPIRIT

After the universal chamber there is another door that leads to a beautiful realm of spirit. It is sometimes referred to as the Void, as nothing dense exists in this dimension. As the door opens you disconnect from your physical body and connect with the spiritual being that you are, so you may sense a feeling of lightness and buoyancy. You can feel a real sense of liberty as you let go your physical form and connect to your spiritual essence.

Within this dimension of spirit there are a number of different aspects or levels and the vibration changes, although all are of love. Because you are coming into spirit through your heart, you are moving into the 'planes of love' – and you are protected from the hustle and bustle of the spirit world that hangs close to Earth, where all forms of spirit can hang about. Only evolved souls, angels, and spiritual and celestial masters reside here, in other words only those spiritual beings that vibrate to the energy of unconditional love.

ANGELS

It is the most amazing feeling to step into a realm of love. Hopefully Earth will be like this one day. The vibration of God's love and energy is so strong that it would blow most of us away, so God created angels to be his messengers and helpers in a form that is closer to the dense form of the human life. Angels answer our pleas for help. If you have any specific requests for healing or assistance, for yourself or someone dear, step into the angelic realms and ask.

Just be aware that the help may not come in the form you expect. Sometimes, for your greatest good and the best

Our hearts are open when we are happy with who we are

result for you, the angels will organise things so that you appear to go backwards before you go forwards. They may present you with further challenges rather than resolving your immediate problem. Trust that your soul's desire and needs, the needs and best advantage for all those involved, are their highest concern. Sometimes the timing has to be precisely arranged and your wishes and prayers aren't answered in the timescale that you think appropriate. You just have to hold faith and trust that all is going to be as it should be, and that when you work from your heart and accept all the love and help that comes towards you, the very best result will be forthcoming.

ASCENDED AND CELESTIAL MASTERS

Let me also introduce to you a great source of wisdom and love that I connect to in the realm of spirit – the Ascended Masters, individuals who have been through their cycle of life and death on Earth and have evolved to the point where they no longer need to come back. Once they have reached this elevated position, won their wings as it were, they have choices how and where they continue their spiritual work, as we don't retire completely when we have finished our Earthly work.

They have the option of being healers and teachers in the spiritual realms, they can do backroom work for the Earth and mankind, or they can have a more direct connection with us and focus on speeding up our evolution. They take more of a teaching role than the angels and they are generous with the wisdom they have accumulated through their Earthly journeys. They are rather like elders of the Native American tradition.

These sages have undertaken the heart work we are now

attempting and have reached the stage of their existence when they are filled with love. It's completely second nature to them to love everyone unconditionally and without judgement. They know everything about you, good and bad. They know all your faults, but they see them from a different perspective. They see them as imprints and wounds that need to be released and healed – no more than that. Rather in the way that a doctor sees a patient as a body that needs curing and doesn't judge character or personality, the Ascended Masters are only interested in helping you heal yourself and reach the same level of clarity and understanding as they have.

MAKING THE CONNECTION

Once you have made your way through this doorway you can assess the wisdom and love of these wonderful beings. All you need is the intention to do so. In fact you can connect to masters and spirit guides – they may be family members who have passed on – at any time or in any place. But you will find it easier and clearer if you travel through your heart centre to make the connection. There are a couple of ways you can do this. You can meditate and speak to them in your head, or you can channel. Let me explain what channelling is.

Channelling the masters

Channelling is a modern word that describes the kind of work that has been going on since the days of the Oracle at Delphi. It is a method of spiritual communication that has been used by holy men and spiritual gurus through the ages. In the past these messages were usually warnings, guidance or portents of the future, and the messengers were called prophets.

Our hearts are open when we share a meal together

Some psychics allow themselves to go into trances and allow spirits to take over their bodies to pass on messages; these we describe as trance channels. Mediums connect to their spirit guides in order to receive messages for their clients.

Today it is fairly commonplace to find people who have opened up enough trust to allow masters to speak or communicate through them. It is not difficult but requires trust and chutzpah, the nerve and the courage to give it a go. I have tried voice channelling – allowing a master to use my voice box to communicate to a group. I found this a little unnerving and haven't been totally successful with that particular form of channelling. I find it easier to sit at a computer and let the evolved spirit or spiritual master dictate while I type. I have received enormous help and wisdom from my own spirit guide, Enoch, and this is the process that I use. It works best when consistently done at the same time of day:

To connect to an Ascended Master for guidance

✧ Surround yourself with white light to shut off outside energy interference and visualise yourself going through the chambers of the heart to the spiritual realm. This ensures that you are on the vibration of love before you start.

✧ Then say either out loud or in your head, 'I am open to receive any messages you have for me.'

✧ Next you can use the symbol below, which I have been given by my spirit guides, to make the connection easier and faster. This symbol opens you to the vibration of wisdom and love that you are seeking. In the air draw the pyramid

---

Our hearts are open when we trust each other

with your finger or hand, starting with the base; then draw the spiral, from the top downwards. It does not have to be exact.

Enoch and his colleagues in spirit are completely committed to helping us transform our world into a more loving place. They cannot do it themselves, but they can assist us and help us to move towards this goal. They don't only use these open channelling avenues to pass information to us, they also, like our spirit guides, fill our heads with ideas and inspirations. They work on a personal level, but their ideals and visions are for groups and for the world as a whole, so the messages are often for groups of people, intended to teach ways in which they can help us improve our world.

Channelling is only as good as the clarity of the channel and it is possible for the information to be affected by any fears, strong opinions and attitudes held by the channel. The most exceptional channel I know is Helen Barton, the mouthpiece for John the Beloved. I love John – he has an incredible sense of humour that pervades his sessions. There are a number of channels who publish the messages they receive on websites. I have listed a few of my favourites at the end of this book. Do read what they say. If it feels good, take it on board; if not, let it be.

Our hearts are open when we confide in each other

THE FOUR CHAMBERS

Here is a schematic that depicts the chambers or temples of the heart as they have been shown to me. I am sure there is a lot more to find out about the spiritual heart, but what I have said should give you an idea of the importance of the heart to your wellbeing and happiness. Only when you open your heart to love can you really live life to its fullest.

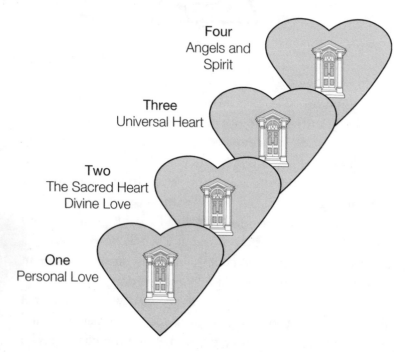

Four
Angels and
Spirit

Three
Universal Heart

Two
The Sacred Heart
Divine Love

One
Personal Love

The Four Chambers of the Heart

OPENING YOUR HEART – LOVE IS THE KEY

I will now take you through a guided visualisation to open your heart. You may like to record it yourself and then play it back so that you can relax and let it unfold, or get a friend to read it out to you. There is a recorded version on CD that you can purchase from my company Ripple – see the back of the book. You can work through this meditation step by step and I suggest you start by doing just that. Afterwards, whenever you feel like healing your heart, feeling more love, connecting to the universe, talking with angels, connecting to your own loving nature or becoming at one with the divine within you, then you can choose the part that suits your mood or need and step into it at any stage.

Here is a symbol you can use to send out the intention that you wish to clear away all barriers and open your heart. It will reinforce your conscious decision to be open to receive love. As you work through this meditation you may feel some discomfort and tightening in your chest, but this will clear later – it is a sign of change in your heart centre.

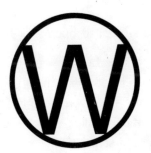

Symbol to Open your Spiritual Heart

Draw the circle first, in a clockwise direction, and then the W, starting at the top left-hand side. Draw three times in front of you, then place your hand on your heart for the entire process.

Our hearts are open when we respect each other

Meditation to open your heart — love is the key

✧ Find a quiet place where you can relax and with time to spare. Close your eyes, drop your shoulders and relax. Hold in your mind the intention that you are now prepared to bring love into your life and let go all restrictions and barriers that stand in its way.

✧ Allow yourself to be a great tree and imagine your roots growing deep into the ground beneath you. See and sense your roots growing deeper and deeper into the ground, connecting you to Mother Earth, and feel yourself getting stronger and stronger as your roots grow deeper and deeper. You are now grounded and secure.

✧ Ask your spirit guides to help you with this great healing process. Don't worry if you don't know who they are — they will be with you.

✧ Now draw the symbol to open your heart 3 times.

✧ Imagine that you have become very small. You walk down the steps that lead from your mind to your heart centre. At the foot of the steps you stand in front of a door. You are standing outside the first chamber of your heart. Push the door open and step inside.

✧ You are stepping into the most beautiful chamber, filled with your love — the love that you give to all those close to you. See a candle glowing in the centre of the room. This is your source of love.

✧ The chamber is filled with all the people who you have

Our hearts are open when we accept each other

allowed to enter your heart. Some are still in your life and some have now gone, but their love carries on in your heart. They are happy to see you; they put their arms around you and bring you to the flame.

✧ They all want you now to receive and absorb the love that you give out to others every day of your life. Allow yourself to receive this love and the love of others. Enjoy some time with your dear ones and enjoy their love.

✧ When you are ready to move forward, you can step through the flame and walk towards another door at the far end of the chamber.

✧ An angel will be with you now as you face this door; it may be covered with locks and bars and barricaded. These are blocks to your ability to move forward. Each one was created after a painful experience to stop love entering.

✧ Are you ready to move forward and open up this door? If so, the angel will help you to dismantle the bars and bolts. As you bring them down, accept who you are and know that all is well – everything that has happened is part of your personal journey.

✧ Bring down the large wooden beam of guilt that blocks the door. Know that all parts of you, black and white, good and bad, are integral to who you are and were necessary for you to form the person you are today.

✧ When all the blocks are down, push open the door – the angel will help. Step forward into a chamber filled with the most brilliant white light. You are now in the chamber of divine love, your sacred heart.

Our hearts are open when we communicate honestly

✧ Allow this light to wrap around you; let the light fill you and accept the energy of divinity that is the very heart of you. Know that you have been created from a creator, a source of great love, and that hence you are a being of great love and a creator. For you are made of the same energy, the same source. Allow yourself some time in this most wonderful temple of love.

✧ When you are ready, step through the chamber to the next door facing you.

✧ This door opens to the universal chamber. The door opens and you see the world. You are able to connect to all of creation. Whatever energies you need at this time are waiting for you – just think of the source of whatever you need and the energy will flow towards you. With your heart open you can receive this energy and allow it to flow through you, filling you with the power and strength you desire.

✧ Stay here as long as you need, then step forward to the next door.

✧ To enter this chamber hold the intention that you step out of your physical form, leave it like a coat and move forward as spirit.

✧ Call for the help you need. The angels and masters will appear to you and give you guidance. They are waiting for you, even if you don't see them. Just accept their presence and open your mind to receive.

✧ When you are ready, you can allow yourself to grow back to your normal size, then step back into the room.

Well done, bless you.

Our hearts are open when we laugh with each other

Daily exercise for opening and balancing the heart centre

To reinforce your intention of opening your heart, you can follow the next short meditation daily.

✧ Close your eyes, touch your heart centre in the middle of your chest.

✧ Visualise a tight pink rose bud. Hold the intention in your mind to open your heart and this rose.

✧ See the petals opening gradually, one by one. Continue until the rose is in full bloom.

✧ Know that your heart is open to give and receive love.

Our hearts are open when we are patient with each other

LIFE OFFERS WAYS TO OPEN YOUR HEART

We have looked at ways to open your heart using intention and visualisation, but there are situations occurring all around you that give you the opportunity to open your heart. You need to be receptive to these situations and see them as opportunities. For example, many natural disasters are opportunities for us to open our hearts in compassion, to empathise with those who have lost family and friends, had their homes destroyed, their livelihoods taken away, and who face disease and suffering.

In the year before I wrote this book we experienced the Asian tsunami, the flooding of New Orleans and the earthquake in Pakistan. These were all disasters that affected thousands and we were brought close to the survivors through our televisions and newspapers. The outpouring of aid and love from all around the world was enormous. The whole of humanity was able to open its heart and feel the pain and suffering of these people just like us, with families and homes. Through our empathy with their loss our hearts opened. We had the opportunity to help by sending gifts and financial aid which gave us the chance to open our hearts without the judgement that often clouds our perception of a situation when war is involved. There were no questions like 'Do they deserve help?' or 'Could they have managed to avoid this situation?' There was no doubt that they needed help and we could give it.

These were events that came to global awareness, but there will be situations in your office, your neighbourhood, school, and so on, that cause hardship and suffering. Any such event can be a chance to open your heart – just as the little boy in Tibet opened my heart.

Our hearts are open when we understand each other

GIVING

Whenever you value another person's need and give some of what you own, you are opening your heart. Whether you give to small or large charities, to individuals, to animals or to help the environment, you are opening your heart. Whether you give money or time you are opening your heart. The act of giving is a spiritual energy exchange and the good feelings you gain are your reward. So be aware that the kind thoughts, kind deeds and assistance you give anyone will return to you as loving energy, and will assist in the healing and opening of your heart.

In Hong Kong I met Dr Cary Rasof, an American who is following his mission in life to help the world's most needy and to create opportunities for others to give. He has given up his lucrative doctor's practice in the United States to travel the world giving medical and spiritual support where it's needed the most. He has been to the most deprived and struggling communities in the world and has offered his skills and his love. Above that he has brought to the world awareness of the needs of others, gently cajoling us to give more where and whenever we can. His website is listed in the Resources section at the end of the book. He plays a similar role to Bob Geldof and Bono, who also give their time and efforts to bringing the needy and the givers together – they do great work in opening our eyes and our hearts. Bless them.

YOUR HEART FLOODS WITH JOY

Certain experiences that we enjoy will actually flood our hearts with love. This rush of love and joy creates a most moving experience, often accompanied by tears. These

Our hearts are open when they sing with love

experiences include great music, beautiful sunsets, the birth of a child, connecting with nature, a wedding, crossing the finishing line first, even seeing your home team win! The energies of joy and awe are the energies of love as appreciation and are powerful forces to open and heal our hearts. If you think back over your life I am sure you will recall such times. Spend a few moments now recalling some of these experiences, remembering situations that opened your heart and filled you with joy.

So there are many opportunities for you to work on your heart opening. We are now going to look at how you can heal your heart, by releasing the pain and hurt of the past and healing any damage that you may be experiencing.

Our hearts are open when we solve problems together

SEVEN

Healing Your Heart

You have made the first major steps to repairing the damage of the past with your intention and commitment, and by visualising the opening of your heart. As you bring down the barriers, you allow yourself to receive and give love. We will now look at ways to heal the scars, mend the heart-break, soothe the pain in your heart and release the imprints from the past, in preparation for welcoming the love you are now open to accept.

LEARNING TO FORGIVE

Several of the wounds that we have discussed and the circumstances that caused them can be healed by similar processes. Forgiving is the first essential step in your journey down the path of healing. It is a MUST for dealing with any issues that come from the past. So if anyone at any time did something to hurt you in any way, you need to forgive . . .

Have compassion for yourself and each other

FORGIVENESS SETS YOU FREE

Through my healing work I have learnt the truth that forgiveness creates freedom. Let me explain this. Most of us have had some experience where we have been treated unjustly, or where we have been hurt by the inconsiderateness or even callousness of someone else. This can hurt deeply, leaving an emotional scar that has long-lasting effects.

However, if you do not eventually forgive the person who hurt you, you will be tied to the situation and therefore the pain for ever. As we have seen, your thoughts are streams of consciousness and energy, and when you continually think of someone you are bound to them by this energy stream like a cord. If you think loving thoughts you create a beautiful bond of love, but if you feel resentment, bitterness or even hate you create dark and negative cords. You are then bound to that person through this negative energy, forcing yourself to relive the hurt over and over again, continuously feeling the pain instead of leaving it in the past where it occurred and where it belongs. The act of forgiveness dissolves these cords. Can you see, therefore, that it is in your best interest to forgive? The only way to let the past go is through forgiveness, or at least total acceptance. Otherwise you prolong the suffering. Forgiving is a gift for yourself as much as it is for the other person. It cures a troubled heart, and it goes a long way to healing a broken heart.

You may struggle with the concept of forgiveness, especially in circumstances where a member of your family has been hurt deliberately by someone, so I suggest you think of great role models who have forgiven the terrible things done not only to themselves but to their loved ones. Here are just a few – you may know others personally.

Do what you think is right and not what other people think is right

✧ **Nelson Mandela.** Nelson Mandela is probably the most famous role model for tolerance, understanding and forgiveness. Held in jail for his political convictions through the majority of his life, he showed nothing but forbearance and tolerance to those who placed him there. It is solely due to his attitude and work that South Africa moved away from apartheid as peacefully as it did. He is a wonderful soul and an inspiration to us all.

✧ **The Dalai Lama.** Another amazing public figure, the Dalai Lama lost his country, Tibet, to an invading force who imprisoned, tortured and killed its spiritual leaders. Yet he holds firm with his Buddhist beliefs of tolerance, compassion and love. He never blames the Chinese; he doesn't stir up hatred for his country's oppressors but continues his work of teaching us all tolerance and understanding. He is a truly blessed man.

✧ **Gee Verona Walker.** Her son Anthony Walker, an 18-year-old A level student, was killed in a vicious and unprovoked assault in McGoldrick Park near his home in Huyton. Anthony was loved and respected, a joy to his family and his school colleagues. It would have been understandable if his mother had felt hatred for his attackers, but she showed the most remarkable grace by saying on television that she forgave them. This lovely Christian woman is a great role model for forgiveness and her amazing reaction showed her up in shining contrast to the young men who killed her son.

All these people have forgiven heinous crimes committed either against themselves or their loved ones. If they can forgive, so can we.

Be kind to one another

BENEFITS OF FORGIVING

It can be very hard to forgive. However, if you can understand why an act that causes pain and anguish has been
committed it may help. Here are some of the reasons why
people hurt others:

✧ They are hurting inside themselves.

✧ They are unable to love due to past experiences.

✧ They have never experienced love and trust, and so
  can't cope with it.

✧ They are mentally ill.

✧ They are seeking attention.

✧ They are fearful of commitment or being attached.

✧ They didn't realise their actions would hurt you so
  much.

✧ They are upset by something you did and they want
  revenge.

You will probably be able to add to this list. Recall times
when you have upset someone. Think back and ask yourself the same question – why did you do it?

The act of forgiving, or even acceptance, releases the
bitterness and rancour of the past. You can then move on
positively with your life. Negative emotions act like poison,
gradually affecting your mind so that you can't sleep or focus
on the positive aspects of your life. You continuously go over
the same thoughts, you have difficulty opening to receive
spiritual love. Finally the poison of those negative emotions

Give each other space to be different

starts to spread into your cells and organs, making you ill.

Once you let go of these negative emotions and forgive, all these symptoms can be reversed. I have seen people totally transformed as they let go. They feel lighter, as if they have released a great weight, a burden they have carried for a long, long time. One woman who released her resentment of her sister-in-law spent the rest of the day vomiting as she purged the negativity from her system emotionally and physically, showing the powerful link between our emotions and physical wellbeing.

Exercise for forgiving and letting go of the past

There are a number of steps to this powerful healing process. Allow yourself a couple of hours for this exercise and take time to rest afterwards to allow the energies to settle. You may find in the following hours or even days that you feel spacy and slightly disorientated; you may experience an emotional rollercoaster until your energies and emotions settle down again. But, and this is the big BUT, you will have changed for the better and you will never be entirely the same again.

Read through the entire process first, then find the time and place and let go . . .

First step — letting go the old emotions

Your heartache will have come with pain and other emotions such as bitterness, resentment, dislike, anger and so on which act as poison. So the first step is to get rid of the poison. Sharing your experience with someone else may help a little, but repeatedly telling your story won't help, for it often magnifies your feelings of outrage. The most effective way to achieve release is to write it down and pass the energy of your emotions to the paper.

You can write anything you feel. Write everything you would like to say but have always considered inappropriate – whether it be anger, shame or love. Nobody else will ever see your writing, so you can say it all without fear of judgement or exposure. Remember this is a healing process for you, a chance to let go for ever the burdens of the emotional pain in which you have been immersed. If you have many issues to clear, focus on one at a time and repeat the process for each situation. If you feel emotional, let the tears flow – crying is another great release.

Second step – burning

Find somewhere safe for the burning ritual. Roll up your paper, light it and as you watch the flames know that all the dark energy you released through your writing is now turning to light. Know that the pain of the past is now turning into wisdom and strength.

Third step – dissolving negative connections

Now to dissolve any negative connections between you and the person you are forgiving. Your endlessly recurring thoughts of anger and bitterness connect the two of you energetically with etheric cords and hooks. These deplete your energy and need to be dissolved before you can move forward.

Be honest with each other without being hurtful

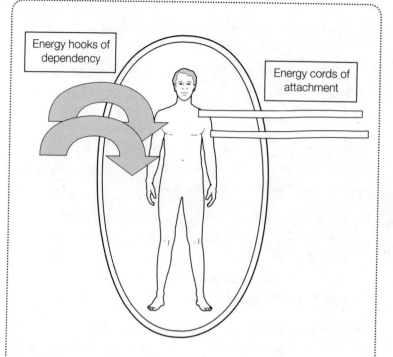

Energy hooks of
dependency

Energy cords of
attachment

In this visualisation you will dissolve the cords and hooks and
forgive. Find a quiet place where you won't be disturbed and
make yourself comfortable. You may like to get a friend to
read the words that follow and take you through this stage of
the process.

✧ Breathe in deeply four times – deep into your solar plexus.
  Drop your shoulders and relax.

✧ See yourself walking up to the gate of a walled garden.
  Open the gate and step into your personal healing garden.
  It is filled with flowers and lawns; it is serene and tranquil.

✧ Start to follow a path as it leads you deeper into your
  garden. You go deeper and deeper until you come to a

Try to see things from the other's point of view

walled courtyard. There is a fountain playing in the centre and roses grow on the walls. There is peace in this inner sanctum. You see a bench and sit down; relax.

❖ Call in now the person or people you wish to release and see them enter the far side of the courtyard.

❖ Between you and each one is a cord. You pick up the scissors that are on the bench beside you. Cut through the cord. The connection is now broken.

❖ See a stream of dark energy now leaving your heart centre; it flows like a river, taking any residual negative feelings away from you. See it flowing into sunlight and gradually turning into light. Keep the stream flowing until it is leaving you as light. Your bitterness has now turned to light and wisdom.

❖ Move towards the person and tell them that you forgive and are setting yourself and them free. All energetic and emotional connections are now released and you are free.

❖ Place your hand over your heart centre and imagine a stream of healing energies flowing from your hand into your heart to ease the pain there.

❖ Gradually you will feel the hurting in your heart subside. Now you can leave the garden in your own time, slowly and gently. Welcome back into the room.

Well done, there is no doubt you will feel a positive impact from this work.

Times are not always a bed of roses, the thorns come with it

HEALING GUILT

....

We will now look at clearing the guilt that can create a huge block between you and the happiness of love. We have all done something at some time that we regret. To heal, you need to first acknowledge what you have done and then forgive yourself. Guilt can become a perennial burden to carry but it is one that you can choose to put down. If you are religious you can ask God or your spiritual masters for grace to clear your karma. Karma is the holding of guilt at a deep subconscious level with the ensuing need to make compensation. Once you have forgiven yourself you release yourself from the resulting perception of debt and bring yourself back into spiritual and emotional balance. It's up to you to forgive yourself and allow yourself the tolerance and understanding that you probably have no problem in showing others. You can be free of the pain and move on.

Accept that you are not perfect and that if you were you would hardly likely be here — you would have reached the zenith of your spiritual development and would be in the heavenly gardens sipping celestial tea or champagne! Accept yourself, love yourself, be kind and forgiving of yourself. Take on board the lesson that the situation and your actions have taught you and absorb it as wisdom.

If you do hurt others consciously, then you will bear the payback of guilt. Remember that guilt is a barrier to allowing yourself to receive love, because you consciously or subconsciously believe that you do not deserve love. It's essential for you to let it go if you want to allow more love into your life. One of the quickest and simplest ways to let go guilt is to speak directly to the person you have hurt and ask their forgiveness. Be honest, tell them how you are carrying the pain of your actions and look for their compassion.

Accept the other person for who they are

Exercise for dissolving guilt

✧ Write down everything you have ever done that shames you. Write each thing on a different line of your paper. You will be coming back to them, so leave plenty of space.

✧ Allow yourself time to consider what you did that left you feeling guilty, and just run through your actions and words one more time in your mind. Don't look for excuses but understand that you were in a different time frame and mindset when you did these things.

✧ See yourself as another person who now needs forgiving.

✧ What did you learn from your actions? Beside each line now write what it taught you and the further ramifications it has had for your life. Take your time over this – look for the positive wherever you can in this analysis. You may find things hidden here that can give you strength and a better understanding of yourself.

✧ Make a vow to be tolerant of yourself and your past mistakes and move on.

✧ Once you have finished with the paper, burn it if possible. As you watch it burn, realise that you are dissolving the pain of the guilt and integrating the energy of the experience into your total being.

✧ Know that the wisdom you gained is a permanent feature of yourself now and that it makes you a better person all round. You have transformed the energy of guilt into wisdom.

In the following meditation you can complete the clearing of your guilt by totally and completely forgiving yourself. If you

Find a balance between freedom and partnership

need to, you will also have the opportunity to ask forgiveness of someone who has passed on.

✧ Find a quiet and relaxing place. Put on some soft and nurturing music. Close your eyes and breathe in deeply four times.

✧ See yourself as a great tree with roots that reach deep into the earth. As your roots go down into the earth, feel the connection to the gentle but strong energies of Mother Earth. Feel the nurturing energies of a mother as her energy comes up through your legs, bringing this loving energy into your whole body.

✧ Now imagine that you are a small child. You are cold and shivering, standing outside a house looking in through the window. The wind is howling and rain drenches you.

✧ Inside it is snug and warm. A mother is sitting on a cosy sofa, gently dozing. You desperately want to be in that warm and friendly place and out of the cold. Here you are lonely and miserable. You know you will be happy and comfortable inside.

✧ You knock on the window and the lady looks up and smiles. She beckons you in.

✧ You see a door and open it and walk inside the room. She immediately gets up and wraps a warm blanket around you and brings you to the sofa.

✧ 'What is the problem?' she asks. You tell her about the guilty feelings you hold inside you. Tell her everything; you can let it all out now – it's safe.

Don't try to be perfect, be true to yourself

✧ She tells you that you are forgiven and tells you to forgive
yourself. Would you forgive this little child? Of course you
would. Would you leave her out in the cold? Of course
not. So let your past dissolve and snuggle up to the warmth
of mother.

✧ If there is someone either living or dead you wish to ask
forgiveness from then visualise them, remember what they
looked like, now imagine that they have joined you in this
room which is a place of healing and peace. Let them also
hug you and forgive you.

All is now well and all is as it should be – bless you. Give
yourself a hug.

Well done, guilt is a hard barrier to shift. You can go through
these exercises any number of times, for some things will
shift quicker than others. The energy of your intention to
let go will eventually pass from thought into your mind and
your spiritual body. One day you will realise that it's
completely gone.

HEALING LOSS

Time is the healer for this heartache and it can take you at
least a year to lose the greatest and deepest pain. Don't deny
the feelings and the memories. Allow yourself to cry as and
when you feel the need. Keep photos of the person you lost
and allow yourself to remember them. If after a year or two
you are still obsessed with memories, then I think you should

have some form of ritual letting go. You can use a method similar to the one in the section on forgiving.

Exercise for healing loss

Step one
Write down your feelings. If you feel any resentment and anger that the person you have lost left you – whether intentionally or not – write it down. Express your feelings of loss and the love you still feel. Write down everything, good and bad. It's all OK, for they are your feelings. Write a letter of farewell. Write about everything that person gave you emotionally.

Step two
Burn the letter or other writing and see your pain transformed into the light of the flames. Your feelings and emotions have been transferred to the paper, so the burning will symbolically transform them from dark to light and will clear them away from you.

Step three
Imagine you are in a beautiful garden. You are drawn to an inner garden filled with pink roses. You see a seat in the garden and sitting there is the person you lost. Walk towards them. Share your feelings with them, then cut the cord between you with love and let them move on.

I mentioned in Chapter 5 how reluctant we are in Western culture to display our grief. We feel too self-conscious to cry in public; even at funerals we hold back rather than letting our

Make time for each other

tears flow. We are too aware of embarrassing people and letting ourselves down. This is not a healthy way to handle grief. Bottled-up emotions of sadness will do us no good at all and the sooner they come out the better. Of course, it's not a question of one good cry and you'll be all right. You will find that the tears well up over and over again, especially when you have lost someone who was very close.

Exercise to let go the emotions of loss

Find a place where you can be private and as noisy as you like without others interfering or being affected. Allow yourself to let rip with your feelings – shout, cry and wail to let go. If you feel like it, beat your chest or the ground. Display everything you feel. Get it out and let it go. Don't be ashamed, don't feel inhibited, for you are the only person who can let this go – no one else can do this for you. Remember that the emotions that you are holding on to are like poisons   –   let them go.

A MEMORIAL

To help you create a closure and to acknowledge that the person you have lost has moved on, you might take comfort from some form of memorial that you can keep close to you. I have a bench in my garden that is in memory of my father, as well as statues for my in-laws, and my mother has a rose planted in her garden for my father. Create a permanent recognition of your shared love.

Make time for your relationship

A RITUAL TO HANDLE REJECTION AND THE WITHDRAWAL OF LOVE

Another barrier we looked at in Chapter 5 was rejection. How can we handle this, and how can we heal the wounds that it caused? Well, first go through the process of forgiveness. What else do you feel? Do you still have a sense of great loss? Take a pink rose to the sea or a river and throw the petals in the water. See this as a closing farewell to lost love.

HEALING THE SCARS OF ABUSE

In Chapter 5 we discussed how scars from sexual abuse can go very deep and how the memories, whether conscious or subconscious, can disturb you for the rest of your life unless you clear them. Some people find that having and nurturing families of their own helps to heal the wounds; others find solace in their work. As a healer I aim to dissolve the imprints and raise your energies to the point where you literally 'rise above it'. Not something that is easy for you to do without help.

Love is the key to healing and the love you find in life will be your healer. So the more open you are to love, the quicker will be your healing. The heart opening process you have already carried out will help you with this. I saw a woman recently who was in great distress. She had been assaulted and molested when she was seven by a close family friend. She and her parents were not close, so she hadn't received the nurturing and loving she needed when it happened. Because most sexual molestation comes from family or extended family, this is a common problem. As she

Make time for fun, laughter and together time

grew older her anger spilt out as rebellion and she lost her schooling. Her self-esteem was already very low through lack of love and her trauma; leaving school without an education compounded this.

She then turned to drugs and chain-smoking as a way to dull the pain. This all had an adverse effect on her relationships – she married and had children, but her condition has deteriorated as her life has progressed and now she feels that she has lost all control of her life, her mind and her emotions. Above all she now needs love, but her behaviour has been driving away her greatest source of love – her family. She has now recognised her need to work on healing and opening her heart to allow the love she needs so desperately to come in.

Abuse leaves in its wake hatred, anger, bitterness, lack of self-esteem, a sense of being dirty and sullied, guilt and fear. So you will need to work through all that I have already covered in this section. But in addition, here is another short visualisation which can help the healing process for you. Sometimes when something bad and shocking happens, you may automatically push a part of your spirit away. It's so painful you reject the part that hurts; this is like forgetting something that happened because facing it is too difficult. And this is what happens in our heart centre when the issue is one of love. In this visualisation you can bring back any missing part of your spiritual heart that has been pushed away in pain.

Exercise to cleanse and revitalise the heart centre

✧ Find a quiet place and make yourself comfortable.

✧ Breathe in deeply – right through all your anxieties and fears, deep into your solar plexus. As you breathe in, know you are breathing in clear and pure air and are cleansing your entire body and mind. As you breathe out, let go all the negativity held for so long within you. See your breath as clouds that rise to the sun and turn into light.

✧ See yourself outside a walled garden – this is your own personal healing garden. Open the gate; enter and close the gate behind you.

✧ You are in a safe and secure place; this is a place of healing. It is serene and tranquil and just for you.

✧ Walk through the garden and enjoy the sunshine and the perfect weather. The birds are singing and the garden is filled with the colour of millions of flowers. Take a few moments to enjoy the scene.

✧ Now take a path and walk deeper and deeper into your garden until you come to a wooded area. You can now hear the sound of water falling.

✧ You come to a small clearing in the wood and you face a beautiful waterfall tumbling in the sunlight to a pool. The sun catches the water and it looks like a cascade of diamonds. A rainbow creates a bridge from the waterfall to the pool below.

✧ You are completely alone, so you take off your clothes and

Keep your doors and windows open to receive love

enter the pool. Feel the cool water washing away all feelings of being sullied by your past. Stand under the waterfall and let the clear mountain water clear away the past for ever. It clears your mind and brings back clarity. You see that you are blameless and that whatever happened is in the past now. Leave it there.

✧ Lie on your back and feel the sun shining on you. Let the light fill your heart and know that the warmth is gradually melting the ice that formed there so long ago. Feel that warmth spreading throughout your entire body.

✧ Out of the sunlight appears an angel. She is holding something in her hand. As she gets closer you can see it is a golden heart. It is your heart fully repaired, with all the missing parts recovered and ready for use again.

✧ She stands over you and drops it gently into your chest. Know you now have a heart that is functioning perfectly and beginning to open so that you can let love in. Love that you need, desire and deserve. Love your soul and your spirit needs to heal.

✧ Spend as long as you wish in this beautiful sanctuary. When you are ready you will find a warm towel waiting by the pool. Dry and dress and in your own time leave the garden. Know you can come back any time you wish.

Well done, bless you.

If your experiences have been very traumatic, like rape or sexual abuse, you may find you get comfort and relief from visiting a counsellor. If you can, find one who comes recom-

Have compassion for yourself and each other

mended by someone you know. I have given some contacts at the end of the book in the Resources section, and I have also included contact details for the support organisations Samaritans, Women's Aid and Victim Support.

HEALING THE SCARS OF DOMESTIC VIOLENCE

If you are still in an abusive situation, please be aware that it is possible to walk away. But you will need support and probably advice, especially if you have a family to consider. It can help talking to a stranger rather than a friend or family member, and an expert will help you draw out the pain and manage it. There are support organisations where you can learn about your rights, what legal aid is available, where you can go with your children in an emergency, refuge and housing options. At the end of the book I have included some helpline numbers where you can speak to someone who will assist you. It might be a good idea for you to use a mobile phone or a public phone for these calls.

Here is the advice that one of the organisations, Victim Support, offers those who are suffering from domestic violence.

WHAT TO DO IF YOU ARE A VICTIM OF DOMESTIC VIOLENCE

Domestic violence is one of the worst forms of abuse. It can include physical assault, sexual abuse and verbal threats. It can also include more subtle attacks such as pressure tactics,

Do what you think is right and not what other people think is right

constant breaking of trust, isolation, psychological games and harassment.

It can affect partners in all types of relationships and can also involve violence between parents and children. If you are in an abusive relationship, there are three important steps you can take:

✧ Recognise that it is happening to you.

✧ Accept that you are not to blame.

✧ Get help and support.

At the end of this book I have given some contacts for emergency help. For your nearest help in your own town or county contact the police or local welfare associations. If you are worried about a friend, neighbour or family member who won't accept your help or advice, just give them a note with the details of the nearest professional help. One day they may just decide to follow up, and they may well be so stressed that they will find it difficult to locate the information for themselves.

Physical violence not only leaves fears and anxieties, but it can leave fearful imprints that lock into our mind and body. These can be difficult to shift, especially when the experience was terrifying or life threatening. You may gain some relief from energy healing and spiritual healing, shiatsu, reflexology, or other healing therapies that clear emotional blocks held in muscles and cells. These therapies can help you release the deep-seated blocks of fear and anxiety that give you nightmares or stop you moving forward in your life.

Be kind to one another

If you find that you continually get yourself into situations where you are being abused, mentally or emotionally, then you may be trapped in a pattern.

BREAKING PATTERNS

You may find that some of the scars in your heart were caused by similar experiences. Do you find that you continuously attract the wrong type of man or woman? Do you see yourself turning good relationships into disasters by following a pattern of behaviour? If you repeatedly find yourself in the same unfulfilling situations, you may need to 'break the pattern'.

TAKE RESPONSIBILITY

You will need to take responsibility for what is happening to you, so first acknowledge that it is only you who are creating these situations – you are not a victim of fate. This acceptance will allow you to be in the driving seat and enable you to make the change that is needed. If you believe everything negative that happens comes from other people, then you will be unable to change your circumstances.

Exercise to break patterns of behaviour and situations

✧ Find a quiet space and relax. Drop your shoulders and breathe deeply four times.

✧ See yourself as a great tree with roots that grow into the

Give each other space to be different

Earth. As the roots grow deep down below the Earth's surface, feel yourself getting stronger. Deeper and deeper your roots go, down through layers of rock and underground streams. You are now completely connected to the Earth and grounded.

✧ Imagine yourself walking along a beach, barefoot on the sand. You can hear the sound of the waves. The sea is blue, the sky is clear and you are at peace.

✧ You have decided to change your life. Hold your intention right now to break the patterns that have been spoiling your happiness. Say out loud that you will break these patterns, and attract people and situations that support you and make you feel good about yourself.

✧ Ahead of you on the beach you see a huge bonfire of driftwood. As you get closer you see a large piece of wood emblazoned with the words that describe your pattern.

✧ Next to the wood is an axe which you use to chop up and break the wood and the pattern into bits.

✧ Now throw them on the fire and know that as they turn into flame, you are seeing all the darkness and limitations of your behaviour, attitude and compulsions turning into light.

✧ Walk away when you are ready, lighter and brighter, and come back into the room to start the rest of your life.

✧ Know that you have chosen love and therefore will receive the love you need.

Laugh together

HEALING YOUR HEART CENTRE

Let's now look at ways to heal the etheric energy of your heart – your heart chakra. After you have opened your heart and worked with different healing processes you may still have some residual pain. To help ease this pain you can use some of these further healing methods.

CRYSTALS

Crystals are natural and beautiful healers that send out their own unique vibration of healing energy. Each type of crystal has a different resonance and vibration. The crystals I have chosen have vibrations that are similar to the perfect energy vibration of your heart. You can use them to magnify the work you are doing to open, balance and heal your heart, and disconnect any negative energy links. You can hold the crystals in your hands as you meditate, wear them over your heart in a pendant, place them by your bed or use them to decorate your room. Remember to cleanse them regularly with sea salt and energise them in the sun.

✧ **Rose quartz.** This is my favourite. It is a pretty light pink stone that polishes up to a beautiful shine and makes great jewellery. Wear a pendant or necklace containing rose quartz over your heart centre and it will send out its healing vibrations all the time, encouraging your heart chakra to come into balance and to heal. I have designed a range of silver jewellery for healing, along with Peace & Harmony pendants based on a symbol for peace and created from rose quartz for love.

Be honest with each other without being hurtful

✧ **Green Aventurine.** This soft green stone is useful for activating and clearing your heart chakra.

✧ **Green Obsidian.** Helps to disconnect the etheric cords and hooks that link you to those you have loved. It also clears and cleanses the heart.

ESSENTIAL OILS

I have worked with the essential oils of flowers and plants in my healing sessions for years. Each flower and plant has its own particular vibration and healing energy. Oil blends have the benefit that they not only smell delightful, but the energy of their distinctive aromas affects our olfactory system; it sends messages to our adrenal glands, which in turn affect our emotions and state of mind. So just by smelling a particular essential oil you can improve the way you feel.

To pass on these powerful healing effects, I started a small company with an aromatherapist friend of mine, Debbie Mulkern. We produce a range of blends for emotional healing. We called the company Ripple; to me this encapsulated in a name the whole concept of healing – whatever positive change we make in our own state will automatically flow from us and affect those around us. I explain how we can activate this expanding flow of spiritual growth and healing energy in my book *The Ripple Effect*.

The plant whose vibration is closest to the perfect state of love, and therefore the most effective in healing our heart centre, is Rose. A bouquet of 24 roses produces just one small drop of essential oil, so you can imagine the power of this oil and the effect it can have on our hearts. Here are the ingredients of our 'Love' blend. You can buy this from us or you can select any individual ingredient and use it

Try to see things from the other's point of view

yourself. Just make sure you buy organic, high quality oils. Otherwise they can be contaminated with chemical sprays or fertilisers, which will affect their energy potency:

◇ **Rose**. This is the flower of unconditional love. It is the key oil for wounds of the heart, filling us with love to assist us to mend our hearts and nurture our souls

◇ **Geranium.** Holds the energy of nurturing, caring and respect, of mother's love. It is one of the ultimate essences of femininity and harmony, helping us to receive as much love and affection as we are prepared to offer.

◇ **Lemon.** 'Liquid light' for joy, lightness and reassurance. It cools the intellect and brings feelings of abundance and positivity.

◇ **Palmarosa.** For flexibility, non-judgement and kindness. Palmarosa's free movement shows us how to be more flexible in our relationships, to accept change and to go with the flow.

◇ **Ylang Ylang.** For tenderness, sensuality and passions of the heart. A well-known aphrodisiac that helps us get in touch with our bodies and emotions, creating feelings of love and unity with self and our loved ones.

◇ **Vetivert.** For the stillness and inner peace found when we open our hearts to love. It has the ability to calm an overactive mind and cool overheated situations. It grounds and reconnects us to the nurturing qualities of Mother Earth, allowing us to feel peaceful, secure, nourished and in balance.

Healing with essential oils

Essential oils can be used in the bath, suspended in water as a spray for yourself or your room, burnt in water in an aromatherapy burner or used in a disperser which puffs the

Times are not always a bed of roses, the thorns come with it

oils into the atmosphere. We have created anointing oils, made by mixing the blends in jojoba base oil so that they can be used directly onto the skin. Here is a ritual for anointing that you can do every morning:

Anointing ritual

✧ Put a couple of drops of oil in the palm of the hand.

✧ With a finger anoint the third eye (the energy centre in the middle of the forehead, associated with our ability to visualise) for the mind.

✧ Anoint your heart centre for the heart and spirit.

✧ Anoint each wrist pulse point for the body.

✧ Rub the remaining oil into your palms.

✧ Hold your palms to your nose and deeply breathe in the fragrance of the oil four times, so that your entire body and all your senses are affected by the aroma and the energy vibrations.

Heart balm

Before we leave the essential oils I would like to tell you about my heart balm. I have been giving workshops for some years called 'Letting go . . .', designed to release the cords that bind us to past love and to heal the pain of heartache and heartbreak. I felt I needed a healing heart balm to help with this pain. On a visit to South Africa I met Margaret Roberts, the country's leading herbalist. I asked her for a

Accept the other person for who they are

herbal remedy for heartache and she made up a recipe for me which we have adapted just a little:

✧ Geranium for nurturing love

✧ Rose for unconditional love

✧ Ylang Ylang for sensual love

She also gave me a bottle of holy water, which had been given to her by a visiting Indian holy man with instructions to send it around the world. So our heart balm contains the oils of love and the water of love. And I have taken it round the world, as we use it in workshops in all the countries I visit!

Roses

You can use fresh roses. Place these lovely flowers by your bed at night so their energies can permeate your room and yourself while you sleep. Red and pink roses are particularly in tune with the energy of love and your heart. They will also act as a reminder to you to focus on your heart – and they look good too! You can dry the flowers when they die and put the petals in your linen drawer.

Exercise: Healing pain with love

I have found this particular healing visualisation very useful for healing a physical pain, a situation that is troubling you, an aspect of yourself, an emotion or attitude, in fact anything you wish to heal. Meditation is relaxing, and because this is self healing it is especially empowering. You may like to record the words

Find a balance between freedom and partnership

so that you can lead yourself through, or you can contact me for a CD (see the back of the book). Don't worry if you cannot visualise; just know that all this is happening to you.

✧ Find a quiet place, free from pets and children. Turn off your mobile and phone. Make sure you are at a comfortable temperature. Sitting is preferable, as lying down may encourage you to sleep.

✧ Close your eyes and take four deep breaths.

✧ Imagine that you are a great tree, like an oak. See your roots going deep into the ground beneath you. You are now connected to the Earth and are secure and strong. Feel and sense the energies of Mother Earth, loving and supporting, coming up your roots like sap rising. They fill your body with energies of strength. You are now totally secure and stable.

✧ Visualise yourself standing in front of a door. You open the door and walk into a beautiful chamber of pink light.

✧ There is a chair in the middle of this wonderful room. Sit on the chair. You are surrounded by a pink mist of love energy. It streams around you and caresses you.

✧ Now focus on the part of you that needs healing. See it as a colour. What colour is it? Is it dark or light? Does it take a form?

✧ Now I want you to take this colour in whatever form it comes to you and hold it and love it. Imagine it is something that you cherish and love. Sit there for some time

Don't try to be perfect, be true to yourself

and watch how your love and tenderness is changing the colour of your problem. Continue to send it healing until it becomes lighter.

✧ Now bring it in your hands to your heart centre, in the centre of your chest. Know that you are going to love this until it's healed completely.

✧ When you are ready, leave the room.

You can repeat this healing process for as long as you like. You should start to feel lighter and the problem should become less intense. Eventually you should start to feel more peaceful.

PRACTICAL STEPS TO RECOVERY

FILL YOUR DIARY

One of the most effective ways I have found for helping loneliness and making a new start is to fill my diary. Sometimes it's better to get out into the world and take part in things, even if they are not absolutely your favourite pastimes – then, as life starts to kick back in and you make new friends, you can be more selective with your diary.

PASTIMES

Here are a number of pastimes that are particularly helpful when you are suffering from emotional pain, or are just lonely because you are in a new place. Some will resonate

Communicate openly and compassionately

and some will be a disaster, but I do think it's worth giving things a go. Unless you try you will never find out what really works for you. I will be talking more about activities to meet people in Chapter 10. Here I will focus on a few that are especially good for your wellbeing.

Yoga

There are many different types of yoga available, some more energetic than others. I personally don't look for a sweat when I go to yoga but a chance to stretch, get back into balance and unwind. Any emotional shock leaves you out of balance and yoga, Pilates and core stabilising exercises will all help to bring you back into line. When you work on physical balance you also come into harmony and balance mentally and emotionally.

Exercise

I am not a great fan of the gym because I prefer to take my exercise outside. However, my stepdaughter, Amanda, is a holistic personal trainer and she teaches stretching exercises that can be extremely beneficial to help release tension and emotions trapped in muscles and joints. Thoughts and attitudes programmed in from childhood can be released as we realign our bodies.

Meditation

Buddhism is strong on meditation and the main intention is to clear the mind – to think of nothing. This calms you down, slows the heartbeat and allows you to release all emotional charge. Most of us find this quite a difficult pastime and it takes some years to master. However, there are alternative methods of meditation that may suit you:

Make time for each other

✧ **Sitting quietly and contemplating.** An old saying goes 'Sometimes I just sits and thinks and sometimes I just sits.' This was the hardest skill I have ever had to learn – doing nothing! Slow down, take time out and listen. Do you rush from one appointment to another, fill your day with projects, leave no time for quiet relaxation? You will find it beneficial to take part in any of these forms of meditation, but really this one is the easiest and you can do it anywhere, at any time.

Just sit, and either close your eyes or stare into the distance and just BE. It can be useful to set off the process with four deep breaths. You may be surprised what inspirations you receive. I have installed patio doors in my office so that I have access to our garden and in the summer I get up from time to time and walk outside just to breathe, take a break and appreciate my garden. I sit on the wall in the sun and do nothing. It's wonderful. Of course, the phone does its best to spoil the peace!

Action: Try doing nothing – stop what you are doing, put down this book and just sit still for a few moments. You choose whether to listen to any thoughts that pop in or you can discard them. It can help to focus on a flower or candle.

✧ **Listening to music with your eyes closed.** No matter what style of music you enjoy, it will be enhanced if you close your eyes. Let the music take you away from your current problems and pain. In my twenties I went through a difficult time when my first marriage broke up, the man I loved left me and I entered into a series of debilitating relationships. When it all got too much and I could feel the tears of self-pity coming on I would go home, take the phone off the hook, be determined to feel sad and get out all the music that made me feel particularly miserable. I would grab the tissues and have a really good cry, and I wouldn't let myself stop until the tears had stopped flowing. After a while I would get bored with feeling miserable and come out of it.

Action: You have to do this on your own – other people will try to talk you out of it and then it won't work. Allow yourself a good wallow! Get out the old photos, play the CDs and allow yourself to cry as much as you need.

✧ **Walking meditation.** My first introduction to this form of meditation was in a wonderful spa in Thailand that focuses on complete and holistic wellbeing. This walking meditation was taught at the sunrise session by a Buddhist monk. Simply move with grace, very, very slowly, taking note of every movement as you go; being conscious of the very effort of moving and focusing on balance and containment. It is very relaxing and peaceful and can be done any time of the day, but is an excellent way to start the day. Now we live in the New Forest in England my husband and I take our dogs for a walk over the open forest every day. We walk for over an hour. Sometimes we talk and discuss things, at other times we walk in companionable silence, sometimes we go alone. I find this the best way to start the day.

Action: Take a walk as soon as you can – anywhere. Just enjoy the very action of walking; see it as a way of relaxing and letting go the stress of your life. Be conscious of everything that is going on around you. If you are in

Make time for fun, laughter and together time

the woods, hear and sense the trees, animals and birds – feel the air and the twigs underfoot. Take a few moments to go very, very slowly, with total consciousness and with all your senses alert.

✧ **Guided visualisations.** As you have probably gathered by now, I am a great believer in guided visualisations for healing all sorts of problems and have recorded several CDs. These are helpful if you find it difficult to shut off from a chattering mind; they give you a focus. You can visit my website, where you can hear a track from each CD so that you can see if they suit you. It's a good idea to find a quiet place for meditation, without interruption from phones and other people. You don't have to sit in any particular position. Just be comfortable, but not so comfy that you fall asleep! Before the meditation, slow down your pulse and show your body that you intend it to relax by breathing in deeply four times. Your imagination is a powerful force that can change things for you and is the communicator between your brain and your subconscious. You can control aspects of yourself by the vision you choose and you can also determine what you attract into your life.

Visit a spa

My favourite way to feel good is a relaxing aromatherapy massage. Any form of deep tissue massage, although not so relaxing, is particularly useful for releasing the stress and negative emotional energies that we hold in our joints and muscles. There are lots of great therapies that focus on drawing out your negativity and clearing energy blocks, including Indian head massage, shiatsu and reflexology. Acupuncture is also a great way to clear blockages in your

Make time to say 'I love you'

energy meridians, the energy lines that flow through your body feeding energy to all your major organs and extremities. I suggest you make a plan to visit a good spa or holistic healing centre and book yourself a healing treatment.

Fun

Whatever makes your heart sing – do it! Laughter is still the best medicine, so indulge in your favourite source of fun and laughter. Life is definitely to be enjoyed and any opportunity to be joyful should be grasped.

I hope you find something that resonates with you in these suggestions for healing your heart. As I have said, healing is not normally something that happens in moments, but with constant focus and commitment you will gradually find that you feel a lightness in your heart as the heartache and wounds are healed. As you work on yourself and your inner issues you will find it easier and easier to receive love.

In the next two chapters we will look at ways that you can bring more love from your existing relationships by bringing down the barriers that may exist between you and those close to you, changing your perceptions and approach to your loved ones and opening yourself to the love that is there waiting to be received.

Keep your doors and windows open to receive love

EIGHT

Healing Relationships

Our journey through life is always beset with obstacles, and in marriage or living partnerships these are up front and in your face. In this chapter we will look at some of the hurdles and other situations that can occur, changing your close and loving relationship into a challenge and a struggle.

For the past few years I have been writing a column in the *Parents' Journal* in Hong Kong. I write a short article each month for couples and answer questions from readers. Here are some of the situations that I have encountered through dialogue with my readers, highlighting the challenges that we can encounter in marriage and long-term partnerships. I offer a number of suggestions for healing and solutions for some of these specific problems that so many of us face.

INFIDELITY

I might as well start with the biggie! It is a huge shock to discover that your partner is unfaithful. I personally faced this with a past boyfriend and it felt like a blow to the solar

Say 'I love you' loud and often

plexus and heart centre simultaneously. I felt as though I had been hit by a truck. It hurts so much because it is betrayal, apparent withdrawal of love, loss of trust, and shame, all in one lethal package. However, if you can withstand the pain then it's a good idea to look at the bigger picture before packing bags and maybe children and moving out.

If it was a one-off – for example your partner slipped up on a night of drunken excess at the office party – maybe your marriage or partnership can be saved. Rather than act in anger, wait a short time until your emotions are a little more under control before you make decisions that can have long-term effects on you and your family. It *is* possible to forgive and move on and it *is* possible to bring trust back – it may take time, but if both of you are prepared to work at it then it could be worth the effort. A friend of mine left her husband and had an affair. After a year she returned and they now have a really fulfilling and happy marriage, as they have let go the past and both are working on the aspects of their marriage that caused the original rift. So it can be done. And if you are close and have a good friendship with your partner, it can be far easier than living alone and taking the emotional and financial strain – especially when children are involved.

If there is no chance of recovering the relationship then be positive about the future. Very often as one door closes a better one opens. I have come across several men and women who were jilted and who have moved on to really fulfilling and very happy relationships. In fact they have found someone who is far more suitable, understanding and loving for them than their original partner. Here is the story of someone who lost a marriage and found love.

Say 'I adore you'

LEE AND STUART

Lee has had a number of challenges in her relationship with the love of her life, Stuart. When they first met, Stuart was getting over a broken relationship with Heather but he soon forgot her as he and Lee grew closer and closer. Stuart enjoyed his nights out with his friends and, despite the fact that he was a bit of a handful at times, Lee went along with him. Her family and friends were critical of his behaviour but she loved him, and his extrovert nature was one of the things that had attracted her to him in the first place. One day Lee found a note from Heather on Stuart's desk. She was distraught and heartbroken to find that they had been seeing each other again. She packed her bags and went to work overseas. But Stuart phoned her every day begging her to return. Eventually he wore her down and she returned, and after a few months they married and had a baby, George. With the birth of his son, Stuart became more settled and Lee tolerated his occasional late nights and boisterous behaviour. When George was four they went overseas for New Year with friends. In the middle of the New Year celebrations she overheard Stuart speaking to Heather on his mobile. She challenged him and he admitted he was in touch with her, but only as a friend and assured Lee that he didn't love Heather. They returned home together, but Lee was so upset that she moved out and it seemed the marriage was over.

Once again Stuart bombarded her with flowers, gifts and phone calls, asking for forgiveness, confirming his love for her and begging her to return. In a healing session, she shared with me the fact that her attitude to Stuart was heavily influenced by her family and friends who said that his behaviour was unacceptable and that she should divorce him. But she

Say 'I respect you'

still loved him. I then asked her a couple of questions. Did she truly love him? She responded fervently. Yes. Could she ignore other people's expectations and influences? Yes most definitely she could. Could she forgive him? Yes she could. Did she want to continue to live with him? Yes she did. I told her to totally ignore everyone else's comments, take hold of her own free will, make her own choice and follow her heart. So she decided that she would go back to him and accept him totally. Since then their relationship has flourished. He has stopped roaming and they spend more evenings going out together as a couple. Because of Lee's honesty about her feelings, her tolerance and her forgiveness, their relationship has had a chance to recover and heal, and her approach has given him a chance to prove to her that his love is sincere and deep. I am delighted to say they are very happy now.

HEALING

If you have been betrayed or jilted you will have a lot of pain and emotion to release. In order for this pain not to block or close your heart, it's imperative that you release all initial pain and anger through tears and any outward display of emotion that comes naturally. Try not to resort to physical violence if possible! Your loss can be as severe and deep a pain as losing someone through death, so you should give yourself time to grieve – and this could take a year before the pain subsides.

Allow yourself to go through the process, give yourself time to wallow and feel the pain and try not to suppress your feelings about your experience. Once the initial hurt is past you can start looking at the positive side of things and see where new opportunities may be waiting for you.

Say 'I appreciate you'

In Chapter 10 I will be exploring ways that you can restart your life and find new love.

THE SHADOW OF THE EX

There are times when an ex-husband or wife or partner can cast a shadow over a new relationship. This occurs very often when you have children and access rights are involved. Sometimes a new partner can become jealous for no real reason other than a feeling of insecurity. Most people feel a certain frisson when the ex is mentioned and it's quite natural to compare yourself. However, remember that you are the current choice and that jealousy can become a nasty intruder into your relationship. This situation needs to be handled sensitively on both sides and is a great opportunity for tolerance and understanding.

It's wise not to show too much open affection to your ex in front of your new partner, but if you have children it's good for them to see that you get along well. Try not to gossip about your ex or assassinate their character, even if you feel murderous towards them – this causes negative energies that can create discord for everyone. If you really do have a lot to put up with, speak about it calmly with your partner and get rid of any emotion by writing it down and burning it (see Chapter 7).

If you are the one who has left a partnership, you may feel guilty and this may cause you to hold on – trying to let go gently as an act of kindness. This doesn't always work as it can raise the hopes and expectations of your ex, and it can upset your current partner too. I think a clean break is kinder in the long run for everyone. When I split up with my first husband it was, as ever, a truly traumatic time for

Say 'I need you'

both of us, but we made a decisive break. A year later we met up and found that our friendship had survived, and we continued to meet and have evenings together. This went on until he met someone new. Then I retired from the scene immediately to avoid causing any problems for his girl-friend – who, I am glad to say, he went on to marry.

Sherry, the daughter of a friend of mine, was having a really difficult time with her boyfriend, Nick. Not because they weren't getting along well – they were very much in love, and although living in different countries, everything was fine. Except for one thing. Sherry, who is normally a well-adjusted and confident young woman, found herself eaten up with insecurity about Nick's previous girlfriend. She would lie awake for hours wondering if she was as good in bed as his ex, or if he still preferred her and was having secret yearnings. Her lack of confidence in their relationship became a real problem, and Nick found it irritating to be asked after sex, 'Was I as good as she was?', 'Do you really prefer me?' and so on. Her fears and anxieties were actually making her frigid, so the very thing that she feared was in fact happening. In a healing session she managed to release the imprint and associated fears from a past life where she had been aban-doned by her lover. Her paranoid fears have now abated.

Suzie still calls her ex-husband to do DIY jobs in her new home and her new partner James is getting fed up with this. She says she isn't yet ready to let go her ex completely and she enjoys this bond with him. If she doesn't let go she could spoil her new partnership and end up losing both men!

HEALING

If you are having a problem letting go a past partner, use the letting-go process from Chapter 7. If you find that you

Say 'I support you'

have unreasonable jealousies, there could be a karmic connection between you and your ex's wife or husband – it's quite
normal for souls in a group to come together in this way.
To release the karmic cords, follow this visualisation.

Exercise to release karmic cords

✧ Close your eyes and relax. Breathe in six times.

✧ See yourself standing outside a lift door. The lift arrives and
you enter. Press the button to take you to the basement.

✧ When you arrive, step out of the lift and enter a passageway.
Walk along this passageway and you will see a door slightly
ajar.

✧ This door will take you to a past life with the person with
whom you have karmic ties. Allow yourself to enter this
lifetime – if you have a problem visualising, just know that
you are in a lifetime with that person. See them either as
they are in that lifetime or, if that is difficult, as they are in
this lifetime.

✧ See silver cords linking you together. Take the cords in your
hands and, one by one, gently break them – holding the
intention of letting go with love.

✧ See the person walking away to continue their life without
bonds to the past.

✧ You also walk back to the lift and return in it up to this
lifetime, free from the shackles of the past.

Say 'I value you'

To cope with an intrusive ex you need to create boundaries in your life and say a firm no to threesomes. If your new partner has children from a previous relationship, open your heart to them but make sure that neither your ex or your partner's ex is included in your new home and life. Be strong in keeping your ex out of your mind – visualise him or her walking through a door that leads to their own road forward and happiness. Send them goodwill and love and let them leave you passively.

'HE HIT ME'

We looked at abusive relationships earlier in the book. But as we are focusing specifically on relationships here, I thought we should take another look at this most negative of situations and see what you can do if you have become caught in the sticky mire of abuse. Both men and women can get themselves into these situations, and it's not so easy to get out as outsiders would think.

One of the problems is that most people who abuse, either physically or mentally, can also put on the charm. They are often very charismatic characters and their dominance makes you feel unable to manage on your own. They deliberately create a dependency or the perception that they are the only one who can help or understand you. From the cases I have seen it's impossible for anyone outside to force the issue. Only when you yourself have decided to step away can anyone really help.

Emotional and mental abuse is insidious and I sometimes wonder if the perpetrator really knows what they are doing. I have friends whose partners put them down in public, ridiculing their input in conversations and generally treating

Say 'I believe in you'

them as second class. Yet these are actually quite kind and considerate people in many ways. I have had boyfriends in the past who have tried to talk me down – not an easy task – and dominate me. I usually found it was those who were insecure themselves who tried this. Bullies often use dominating tactics, bluster and noise to build up their own confidence, hiding their own fears and low self-esteem.

JENNIE

Jennie, a dear friend of mine who is a bright star, a successful and confident character, had a husband who always mocked her, found fault with her in public and generally belittled her. John, her husband, was a quiet, meek, unremarkable man. I asked her if he was as dismissive of her when they were on their own and she said not nearly so much. I think it was his need to seem brighter than her that made him try to dominate her in public. His mother had brought him up alone for the first years of his life while his father was away at war, and she had been a strong character who spoilt him. I believe when he chose Jennie as a partner he was doing what many people do – marrying a mother or father figure. He then tried to push her into the role of his mother – wanting her to be a good cook, and so on – and nagged her when she fell down on his expectations.

So if your partner has issues that need healing, what about you? How can you cope?

HEALING

If the abuse is mild, you can put yourself into a bubble of light – visualise yourself within an egg with thick walls and know that whatever negative words are directed at you will

Say 'I trust you'

bounce off the walls. Don't get into arguments. If my husband puts me down or argues with me in public – and he does sometimes when he gets excited – then I just let it fly over my head. If I think it's worth mentioning later I just point out that I don't really appreciate that kind of treatment. A blazing row creates two losers.

If the abuse is bad then you need to find professional advice, as I mentioned in Chapter 7, in the section 'What to do if you are a victim of domestic violence'. Keep firmly in your mind that what is happening is not your fault, that you choose and can receive love – true love – that does not come packaged with abuse, dominance and cruelty. Remind yourself that you are the only one that can change the situation. Your partner cannot, for I can almost guarantee that you cannot *heal* him or her. Concentrate on healing yourself. Ultimately, the only way to resolve the situation is to step out on your own, seeing yourself as a victor not a victim.

'I CAN'T LIVE WITH HIM AND I CAN'T LIVE WITHOUT HIM'

It's possible to get involved with a person in a love-hate relationship, where your characters are constantly at odds with each other yet there is a great bond that holds you together. The connection that holds you could be karmic – in other words, you may have been together in a past life and had a powerful connection in that life such as great love or deep affiliation.

WILLIAM AND SUE

William and Sue have a relationship like this. They have been

Say 'I love you as you are'

trying to get together for years. Every time they move in together something major comes up between them that splits them apart. They find it almost impossible to live together, but once apart they pine terribly for one another and spend hours on the phone. We have had many sessions with both of them, resolving and clearing their past connections, and the last I heard their fourth attempt to live together is now working! For some, happiness comes when they eventually break away and marry someone else despite the pull.

Alternatively, you could be held together by LOVE! It is possible to find someone's personality and character very difficult to manage and live alongside, while their soul and heart are so loving and generous that you are drawn to them. In this case you will need to be tolerant of the niggles and habits that upset you and learn to live with them, just as Katharine Hepburn humoured the crotchety Henry Fonda in the film *On Golden Pond*. I can tell you that after a while you become immune to things that in the early days of co-existence can drive you up the wall. Generally speaking, we have to put up with a number of irritations and personality challenges when we live close to someone, but if the love is strong and we can exercise tolerance, they diminish in importance.

HEALING

If you believe you are connected and drawn to someone by karmic cords you can use the visualisation to release karmic cords (see page 155). If the bond from the past is very strong and is held by a vow, for example a vow to be together for ever and ever, then you will need to dissolve the vow to release the karmic connection. A vow can be released by the following simple process, which will work whether the vow is one you recall or one from a past life.

Say 'I love you completely'

To clear a vow

✦ Find a quiet place and relax.

✦ Focus on the situation that you wish to heal and the person involved.

✦ Say 'I release and dissolve with love all vows that no longer serve me.' Repeat another three times, saying four times in total.

✦ Say 'I release all ties to the past that no longer serve my highest good – I let them go with love and forgiveness.' Repeat another three times.

'HE ACTS LIKE MY FATHER'

Overwhelming love and attention can manifest as 'knowing best' like father or smothering love like mother. Whether from man or woman this can be great at times and make us feel needed and childlike, but too much of it can be claustrophobic. If you overwhelm your partner with protectiveness and too much fussing, you can drive him or her away. I don't think anyone likes to be smothered, dominated or controlled, even in the name of love. After a time you will either give up your spirit and succumb to the dominance of your partner or leave.

HEALING

If you are the smothered one, you need to discuss the

problem with your partner. If you are the one doing the smothering, I suggest you start by acknowledging what you are doing, for you will drive away the love you so desire if you are not careful. Look for the signs. Do you do any or all of the following?

✧ think of everything for your partner – choose clothes to wear, book hair appointments, cut their nails, wash their hair, cook all the meals, do all the ironing

✧ control the money and the spending

✧ book all the holidays and choose the destinations

✧ ring up all the time to check 'are you all right?'

✧ use the words 'I was worried about you' more than once a year

✧ make your partner the centre of all your activities

If you see yourself in this role then rein back a little. You can still love and care, but your behaviour will either over-power or irritate and as you advance so strongly you may well drive your partner away. Giving love is one thing, but completely enveloping someone with affection can be counterproductive.

'I GAVE AWAY MY BABY'

The loss of a child can leave deep wounds and emotional trauma that may destabilise a relationship. I have two friends who had their babies adopted. Even now, as they come through their fifties, they are feeling the after-effects. Neither

Say 'I cherish you'

of them has a long-term relationship and I suspect that they have both suffered issues of guilt. Both were expecting babies in the days when there was a definite stigma associated with being a single mother. The cultural pressures on a young woman who finds herself in this predicament can be immense.

SUSAN

Susan was a young girl living with her parents in a mining town in South Africa. It was an Afrikaans society which valued the family and 'good living' very highly. When she became pregnant she was told she must have the baby adopted. No other option was offered and she was bulldozed down that route by her family and the community. Unmarried mothers were scorned and disrespected, and at the birth she was assisted by a junior doctor still in training. It seems he was overzealous with the forceps and her baby was born disabled – although she was not aware of this at the time as her little girl, who was named Julie, was immediately taken from her.

Disobeying the rules, Susan crept into the nursery to say goodbye to her daughter before she left. Years later she found out that her daughter had cerebral palsy and in a heartbreaking meeting they were reunited. The people who had adopted Julie had handed her back when they realised that she was disabled and she had spent her entire life in care. As a little girl she had been placed in a Catholic orphanage where she had suffered badly at the hands of strict and unsympathetic nuns. Susan is now close to Julie and they are bonded as a family, but her daughter's issues of abandonment and her own guilt still come to the surface from time to time.

Say 'I love you' loud and often

HEALING

If your partner has lost a child through abortion, adoption or separation, you will need great patience and understanding when the question of having more children is raised. Sometimes the outcome of the trauma is so severe that even when the woman chooses to have a child, it's difficult for her to conceive. Our emotions can affect all aspects of our body and the guilt and pain can act as a block to fertility. If you are the one who lost your baby, you will need to spend a lot of time on clearing and healing your guilt (see Chapter 7). If your child was virtually forced from you, as in Susan's case, you will need to tackle your resentment and anger (see the forgiveness healing in Chapter 7).

'MY FATHER RAPED ME'

Being sexually abused when a child or teenager can have a severe long-term effect on how we relate to others. Issues of distrust, fear, guilt, shame and low self-esteem can come between you and love. Rape at any age, of course, will leave deep wounds and will need sensitive consideration from all those around you. You may suffer from nightmares, panic attacks and other anxiety- and fear-driven repercussions which can put a strain on a relationship.

It takes lots of perseverance and understanding to live with someone who has deep emotional wounding, for it's hard to keep patience and to watch someone you love go through emotional hell. Your own heart will feel pulled apart as you see your loved one's pain. If you are the one who was abused, understand that it's difficult for someone who hasn't been through the experience to fully understand the issues you

Say 'I adore you'

are battling. It's essential that you get help with your healing and choose a way ahead that is filled with love, rather than isolate yourself inside or outside a relationship.

HEALING

We have looked at the agencies and professionals that are there to help and I have given some contacts at the end of this book. If you want to have a fulfilling and loving relationship, you will need to work on healing your wounds. It is possible to heal even the worst situations. There are several autobiographical accounts around just now that share horrific experiences of childhood abuse and their authors' ability to overcome it and make a life. One I found to be filled with hope is *A Child Called It* by Dave Pelzer. Like him, I have seen many people who have suffered severe wounding but who have come through successfully to establish great loving relationships. Above all, hold the intention to value yourself and to be open about your feelings. If these are suppressed, they will fester and fester, becoming the barrier to the very love you need and crave to help you heal your scars.

'MY PARTNER IS A WORKAHOLIC'

It is not unusual these days to be married to or living with someone who is devoted to their work – it's not as bad as having a mistress, but sometimes it seems like it! As you can gather, I speak here from experience. My husband adored his work and worked from 8 am to 8 pm for years, in addition to reading reports in the evening, dealing with evening and weekend telephone conversations, travelling on Sundays and making trips overseas that lasted from one to three weeks

Say 'I respect you'

at a time. I personally found it liberating and used the time to follow my own work dream. However, I know that for some their partner's absence can be a real burden; it can break a marriage. If a husband or a wife is neglected for too long, there is the danger that they will look elsewhere for the companionship and affection – let alone the passion and sex – that they are missing at home.

HEALING

If you are a workaholic I suggest you focus on balancing your life with your partner, with your children if you have them, and with relaxation and personal pursuits. It is difficult, but I recommend you keep your horizons beyond the office. Make sure you woo your partner – either sex can be wooed, of course – as you will have to work extra hard at keeping your relationship together. Make time for each other – my husband Tony and I took lots of short breaks together and I insisted that we went out to dinner at least once a week for valuable time together, although I am sure he would rather have slumped in front of the TV.

If you are married to a workaholic, make sure you keep creating these opportunities and without nagging, insist on spending time together. And find a life of your own! It's essential you don't sit at home and stew, waiting for your partner to come through the door, as this can become a downward spiral. Take up as many commitments and interests as you can and keep yourself busy and involved. If you are living a fulfilling life you won't be putting pressure on yourself, your partner or your relationship. See the benefits and maximise them – use the freedom to your own advantage.

Say 'I appreciate you'

'WE CAN'T HAVE CHILDREN'

Issues about children can be another pressure point in a marriage: whether you want children and whether you can have them. It really is a good idea to decide before you enter a serious and committed relationship whether you want children or not. It can be most distressing to find further down the line that your partner's views differ from yours. What can you do if one of you wants children and the other doesn't?

TESSA

Tessa married Doug, a man older than herself who already had a son from a previous marriage. She was approaching forty and her biological clock was ticking fast. She wanted a family, but Doug felt that he was too old to start another family – he was concerned about the age gap between him and any youngsters they would have. After a couple of years of disharmony on this matter they decided to let fate play its hand. As it turned out, so far she has not conceived, although she had one miscarriage. She feels a lot happier letting go her anxiety about having children and is now prepared to go with the flow. He too is happy to accept what turns up.

Tony and I found ourselves in a similar situation. Although we tried to have a baby when we married it didn't happen. We left it to fate and I have never felt any pangs of regret. Personally, I don't believe it necessary to have children to enjoy a truly fulfilling marriage or life – some of us have just not planned to have them as part of our divine life mission. However, children do bring joy and bonding to a couple. As you create a family, you create a future, and children can be great healers for those who are a little

Say 'I need you'

self-absorbed. I appreciate the anguish that couples go through when their desire for a child is unfulfilled.

HEALING

If you want a child and your partner doesn't, you should consider whether the lack of children would be devastating for you. If so, then find a partner who shares your expectations before it's too late. Resentment is a destroyer of marriages. This is a big issue and if you cannot agree you have an unstable base for your relationship. Discussion and openness are essential. Please don't just sit around moping about this, but bring it up and talk it through.

If you are having difficulty conceiving, follow your dream and have all the treatment on offer. If you have a medical reason for infertility you may consider adoption – there are many children in the world who need a loving home. I visit Aids Baby Homes in South Africa, who are desperate to find parents for their little abandoned orphans.

I have done a lot of successful healing with women who want children, for often the root cause is an emotional block based on fear. I have also come across several women who had made a vow not to have children in a past life, so I have included this in our healing session overleaf.

Say 'I support you'

Symbol for fertility
Draw from top to bottom, adding the dot last.

Visualisation for improving fertility

✧ Draw the fertility symbol in the air three times, then place a copy of it in front of you.

✧ Drop your shoulders and breathe in deeply four times and relax.

✧ Keep your eyes focused on the symbol. Know that this represents new beginnings. Know that you can be and will be open to new beginnings and birth.

✧ Allow yourself to release all fears of the responsibility of having children. Say out loud, 'I release all anxieties, fears and concerns about taking the responsibility of a child into my care.' Say this three times.

✧ Let go all vows from the past that may be blocking your fertility. Say out loud, 'I release and dissolve all vows that may be preventing me having a child.' Say this three times.

✧ Visualise a new shoot emerging from the ground and growing into a beautiful flower.

Say 'I value you'

✧ If you are a man, say 'I am open to create new life with my love.' If you are a woman, say 'I am open to receive new life within me.'

✧ Now on a blank piece of paper draw the fertility symbol three times and hold the intention of conceiving a child.

'I'VE GOT A HEADACHE'

Sexual problems can destroy the best relationships. There are many reasons why the sexual aspect of a relationship may not work. A man who has been dominated by his mother can struggle to feel equal in bed with another strong woman; abuse can leave bad memories about sex; low self-esteem, redundancy, fear and worry about work or money can all have an impact on your sex drive.

Sexual drives vary of course, and give and take is needed if you have vastly differing appetites! It's important to keep working on this and also to find variety in your sex life. You can easily get into a predictable pattern after the first couple of years together and it's equally easy to be 'too tired' to make the effort. Surprise each other – do something unexpected, dress up and seduce each other from time to time, choose a different time of the day or get out into the country for a change. Weekend breaks away from your normal environment can give you a lift. Women enjoy being wooed in a romantic manner – and gifts and soft words go a long way to awakening the zest, gentlemen! And remember this is a relationship issue. If you are both feeling that cuddles are better than sex these days, enjoy the cuddles and forget the sex.

Say 'I believe in you'

HEALING

See sex as an opportunity not only to fulfil desire but also to gain a special and deep closeness with your partner, a chance to share and please. If you have a serious impotency or frigidity problem do get professional help. Don't be shy to try Viagra to help revitalise a flagging drive. These days it's also quite acceptable to ask for counselling for these concerns. Counsellors are understanding and will maintain confidentiality.

There may well be a deep-seated emotional difficulty behind the impotency – dig deep and address any fear or trauma that might be hiding behind the problem. Here is a visualisation that I used for a friend of mine whose husband hadn't approached her sexually for two years. The night after she performed this meditation they had a great romp!

The passionate link

✦ Close your eyes. Drop your shoulders and let your body go soft. Breathe in and out deeply six times and as you do allow your entire body to relax; let go the tension in your arms, legs and shoulders.

✦ Think of the person who is special in your life. Visualise yourself in a boudoir – a bedroom for love. Take a moment or two to relax in this amorous love nest.

✦ See your partner in this room with you. If you are a woman, focus on your sacral chakra (the energy centre below your navel), the source of your creativity and sexual activity. If you are a man, focus on your root chakra (at the base of your spine, between your legs).

Say 'I trust you'

✧ Now visualise a green cord linking your chakra to that of your partner. Know that this is bringing you together passionately and with ardour.

✧ Visualise the hot and passionate sex you will be having later!

✧ If and when you can, pull yourself away. Return to the room. Good luck!

PROBLEMS WITH PARENTS

Mother-in-law, father-in-law . . . parents in general can create havoc if they get too close or interfere too much. However, it takes diplomacy and tact to tell your partner that their parents are creating a problem. In some countries it's quite normal for a young bride to move into her new husband's family home and culturally acceptable to share with in-laws. However, everywhere I visit I hear stories of problems with parents and in-laws – even in Asia. For whatever your cultural background, it is difficult to share a home with another family unit.

In the West we have broken up close-knit, intimate family life and tend to be more comfortable living separately and independently. But this has its drawbacks, as lonely young mothers have found – we have to manage without the on-tap support group of the extended family. Your parents can add a wonderful dimension to your family and provide background support for your marriage, but if they are overpowering they may try to impress their views and ideals on you, make too many demands on your time or drive a wedge between you and your partner.

Say 'I love you as you are'

The way you are treated by your parents in childhood can leave lasting wounds that you may take into your relationships. Judy, a young woman I saw recently, told me her mother would say of her in her hearing that 'She was the ugliest baby I have ever seen.' Madeline, a forty-year-old I met in South Africa, told me that when her mother died she was sold to another family for a bottle of brandy. A negotiation that took an hour to complete and has taken Madeline a lifetime to heal! Many of my clients have heard all too often the words 'After all I have done for you . . .', usually spoken with reference to the everyday responsibilities involved in their upbringing. Verbal putdowns can create a huge burden of guilt onto children – for being a nuisance and burden to their parents. This type of verbal and emotional cruelty from your parents – whether mental or physical can hang around in your consciousness for a long time. It destroys your self-esteem and creates wounds that make your heart either fragile and needy or closed and cold. All such wounds need healing before you can have a deep and balanced relationship.

HEALING

If you have been hurt by your parents, you need to work through all the exercises to open and heal your heart and to achieve forgiveness. If you have problems with manipulative or intrusive parents, then you need to create boundaries between them and your family. Boundaries are strengthened by your determination not to be hurt or upset by the parent concerned.

Be strong about the number of times you or they visit. Be firm that you want to bring up your children to follow your rules. Don't listen to gossip about your partner, and ask your parents to stop running him or her down. Show your

Say 'I love you completely'

love and support for each other and don't take sides with parents or in-laws who try to drive a wedge between you and your partner.

Keep talking to your partner, and without criticising his or her parents make a plan together to manage the situation. This is a great chance to test tolerance and openness. If your partner is unsupportive of you, tell him or her how it's hurting you. At the end of the day you want a partner who is supportive and loving. If they are not, you have something to think about!

ILL HEALTH

Ill health can bring you closer to your partner. Tony needed me more than at any time in our marriage when he became ill – it can be a chance to bond and to show your love and support. However, if one of you becomes chronically ill or disabled, the role of constant carer can become a major challenge to your relationship. I have seen how it can drag both partners down, creating resentment and a feeling of claustrophobia – you may be trapped at home, needed all the time, so that you cannot have free time to yourself. This will be a test of your love and your ability to show empathy, patience and tolerance, but it will also test whether you are still looking after your own needs and wellbeing. It is easy to give so much of yourself to someone you love that you ignore your own health and happiness, relaxation and fulfilment, spiritual and emotional needs.

If you are the one who is ill, recognise that your body is reacting to imbalances that start at emotional and spiritual levels and that you are crying out for love energy – emotionally and physically. Spend some time looking deep within

Say 'I am here for you'

you to see what is the root cause of your illness and what is out of balance in your life. It may be genetic, it may be a virus you have caught. Some emotional disharmony can be found at the root of most illness. As you work through your intentions of opening to love, you will find that your body will respond too. For all of you is connected and all is energy.

HEALING

A lot has been written about care for carers in the last few years as so many people are now ill at home. Do everything you can to find support outside of your marriage and take up any offers for help – don't think that you have to be the only one to care for your partner. Your love will have a greater chance of surviving if you take as much pressure off yourself as possible.

Leave the guilt at home if your partner becomes clinging and tries to stop you taking time off. Gently explain your own needs, for it's easy for the chronically ill to make the universe their bedroom and then become the centre of that universe. This is natural, and it isn't their fault, but you don't want to feel completely trapped. It's essential that you find time for yourself – then you can come back to your role of carer with love and affection. See a sick partner as a great opportunity to show love and affection, a chance to bond through your caring.

One of the problems of caring for someone with a long-term illness is the frustration of having to stand back, unable to make the person better. So use natural energy healing. It doesn't need any special skills, just love and the intention to help another person. Follow this simple visualisation:

Say 'I cherish you'

Exercise to strengthen healing energy

✧ Find a quiet place where you can relax with your partner. In this exercise you will be following the same inner journey you took when you opened your heart in Chapter Six.

✧ Close your eyes and visualise yourself surrounded by violet flames flickering around you. These will prevent you from picking up any negative energies from the person you are caring for.

✧ See steps before you and follow these down to the door of your heart. Step into your heart centre. Walk through all the first three chambers, then at the door of chamber four stop and call in the angels and your spiritual guides to help you.

✧ Draw the symbol below in the air three times. This will send a message to the universe, to your spirit guides and angels, and they will send the healing energies of love and compassion that will pass through your hands.

✧ Place your hands near or on your partner and allow the loving energies of healing to flow into them.

Healing Symbol

Say 'I love you' loud and often

Draw from right to left and finish with the dot. Repeat twice more. The energies of love and compassion will now flow from your hands. Use for yourself or others.

If you are the one who is sick, don't take your partner for granted. Keep telling them how much you love and appreciate them – praise and affection goes a long way to ease the slog of nursing.

MONEY WORRIES AND PROBLEMS WITH WORK

Financial concerns are the big bad wolf of marriage. I read somewhere that money is the number one cause for a second marriage to break up, and I can believe it. Second marriages are often under the strain of stepchildren, ex-partners and alimony fees. Couples argue about money – when to spend and when to save, and what to spend their money on: 'You are spending more than me', 'I earn more than you', and so on.

Financial worries can eat away at the foundation of even the best relationship. Redundancy and difficulty finding work can bring depression and loss of self-esteem, especially for men who for so long have occupied the traditional role of hunter-gatherer – or at least of major wage earner. In these days of balance and equality between male and female, it doesn't matter who brings in the money. But it can still be difficult to step into roles that break tradition.

Say 'I adore you'

HEALING

Your forbearance, tolerance and understanding are being severely tested here. Marriage is a place for compromise, so use your big heart to avoid arguments and your faith to trust that you will receive all the abundance you need. As you open to love, you are opening to love energy in the form of money and abundance in all you need. When you are shut down and the barriers are up, you shut down to prosperity and the blessings of life. Keep working on your heart opening exercises and know that you are open to receive money, a good job, prosperity and financial security.

The symbol below can be used for bringing abundance and prosperity. It sends out the message to the universe that you are ready to accept love in the form of prosperity. Draw the symbol and visualise the form of abundance that you want. Visualise yourself receiving the money or a regular income. When I want to enforce my need for financial support I visualise golden coins falling into my lap or see someone presenting me with a cheque.

Abundance Symbol

Draw three times from right to left, drawing the line last.

Say 'I respect you'

MIXED RELATIONSHIPS

....

When we create a partnership with someone very different from ourselves – different in culture, different in age, different in race or religion – we may come across new challenges.

SIMON AND JUNE

Our friends Simon and June are from opposite sides of the world: Simon is a Scot and June is a Hong Kong Chinese. I think they are a perfect example of how differences can work well together. He is a typical alpha Scottish male – no elaboration needed there – and she is a gentle, quiet but strong Chinese lady who has managed to adjust well to Simon's life of expat businessman.

She has learnt bridge and golf and excels at both. She has expanded her outlook and her abilities to cope with the challenges that a life on the move, changing country every few years, has thrown at her, while holding strongly onto her identity and her own interests. She plays golf in the day and mah-jong in the evening! She has taken all the opportunities her life with Simon has offered; rather than sitting and moaning about the difficulties of her marriage and lifestyle, she has embraced them and enjoyed them.

Simon in turn has adapted to the need to be near her family whenever they can, since close family bonds are much stronger in Asian cultures. They have taken their differences and created a rich and full partnership.

HEALING

See your marriage as a great adventure and a chance to learn more about life through gaining different perspectives. Enjoy

Say 'I appreciate you'

your differences rather than criticising or trying to change each other. Find the fun in diverse interests, habits, food, social experiences, and learn from each other. Use your relationship as an opportunity to bridge the gaps that grow between cultures and races. Your bonding will reflect out to the world that the base of every relationship, no matter where we start our life, is love.

If I have missed a challenge that you may be facing in your relationship, I am sorry. Each of us will find that the obstacles and difficulties that we face in life will affect us differently – one person's blip is another's mountain. See these hazards as what they truly are – challenges. And challenges are made to stretch us and give us the opportunity to learn new and smarter ways to cope with life. Be like the river and flow around the obstacles, rather than try to wash them away with force. Be smart and flexible, and you will be able to overcome the challenges and keep your love constantly alive. Remember to keep expressing your feelings, keep the door open and the communication of love active.

Let's now look at how a positive approach can improve any relationship.

Say 'I need you'

NINE

A Positive Approach to Relationships

How can you improve your current relationships and make them more loving? In this chapter we look at ways that you can improve your relationships, including those that are already working well. Are there things you can do or say that will bring you closer to the ones you love? Do you inadvertently sabotage your relationships or create chasms between you and those your love? We will look in this chapter at how you can mend these rifts and bring more love into all your relationships. We will also look at the most important relationship of all – your relationship with yourself. Because if that doesn't work, then every relationship you enter will be difficult and challenging.

Healing yourself is a long-term project and one that never ends as far as I can see. There is always something we can do to improve our levels of understanding, self-love and well-being, and you will find that as you become more positive and stronger in yourself, it will be easier for you to open yourself and be responsive to love.

Remember to have fun

PERSONALITY AND CHARACTER

....

Marriage and close living relationships offer the environment for testing our ability to love. They also give us the opportunity to allow our love to flourish, to grow from passion and desire into devotion and unconditional respect. But our characteristics, attitudes and personalities are all reflected and magnified within the confines of a close relationship.

If we have emotional wounds, they may create challenging behavioural patterns and attitudes. Sometimes these are not easy to manage and they will be brought to the surface by the close proximity of lovers, family and close friends. So close relationships also provide testing grounds for our ability to develop and heal ourselves, for we cannot heal what we don't either understand or acknowledge. Once we are aware of any damage we are suffering then we can do our best to heal and restore our inner balance and harmony. It's essential to be honest about yourself, whether in a relationship or not, as denial simply allows old hurts and prejudices to fester inside. And they will eventually turn to poison, which comes out as anger, intolerance, low self-esteem and the myriad issues that our past experiences may throw up for us in our earthly journey as human beings.

Some of your attitudes and mindsets are inherited from your parents, some come directly as a result of your own past experiences. And there are some that I believe come with your soul – your spiritual self that comes back to Earth time and time again in order to develop and grow. Strength of mind, determination, bravery and tenacity are just some of these characteristics. In contrast, fear and anxiety, anger and impatience are often the result of past experiences from this lifetime or previous lives. But however they arrive and

Enjoy, compromise and really work at your relationships

whatever their source, negative attitudes and emotional states are barriers and hazards to a good relationship, for they test the love of your partner, family and friends. There is only so much that a person will tolerate before the love is destroyed.

Let's look at some of the common negative characteristics you may bring to your relationships or face in them. To heal these negative tendencies we need to shift them in a positive direction. Some you can heal and energise to make them attributes and strengths. For others, you can shift the perspective to make them a powerful force instead of a weakness. So it's not about cutting out, destroying, eliminating, detaching from or disliking an aspect of yourself – it's about loving it and bringing it under control to the point that it becomes positive.

Negative characteristic	Positive characteristic
Impatient	A 'make it happen' personality. A doer. Someone who gets on with things
Nagging and nit picking	Motivating
Negative and gloomy	Positive and uplifting
Possessive and jealous	Showing loving concern and caring
Self critical	Self aware and knowing
Unfaithful	Faithful and trustworthy
Lazy	Relaxed and chilled

Remember, nobody is perfect and the grass isn't always greener

Intolerant	Tolerant and understanding
Angry and volatile	Passionate – a world changer
Selfish and inward looking	Self respecting
Emotionally and mentally abusive	Loving, accepting and respectful
Childish and insecure	Confident and independent
Unreliable and forgetful	Grounded and dependable
Reclusive and moody	Thoughtful and gentle

By using the following visualisation you can see your negative traits and send them love – see them becoming The Best as they grow positive and strong.

Visualisation to bring strength with love

✧ Write down all aspects of your nature that you would like to change.

✧ Close your eyes and relax. Breathe in deeply four times.

✧ Visualise yourself as a mountain. Feel the rocks that make up your base deep inside the Earth. Sense the strength that you radiate with your head in the clouds and your feet in the Earth.

Do what you think is right and not what other people think is right

◇ Focus on the aspect of yourself that you wish to change
   – send it love by holding the intention that it be beneficial
   for you and others.

◇ Touching your heart, know that this aspect of you moves
   into your heart to be loved. Acknowledge the positive
   aspect of this trait.

◇ Now visualise yourself with this positive trait in action and
   see the good that comes to you and others from its
   strength and power.

BACH FLOWER REMEDIES

Bach Flower Remedies are natural essences of plants that
can help you to subtly modify your personality and character. They can help you bring yourself back to the centre
position between the extremities of behaviour that can challenge harmonious relationships, peace of mind and self-
acceptance. They have a gentle power and give you the opportunity to make changes within yourself, offering the fulfilment
that comes from self-responsibility and the use of self-healing
processes.

The remedies are created by combining the essence of
plants and flowers with natural spring water and are taken
orally. As a medical doctor, Edward Bach believed that the
way to return to happiness – whether from shock, terror,
loneliness or distress, major or minor – was to consider the
whole state of the patient he was treating, rather than simply
the physical symptoms they exhibited. He discovered in
flowers the resonances of the conditions he found in his
patients. By distilling the essence of certain flowers, he

Never go to bed without being at peace with each other

believed, and by choosing the right ones for the state of being in which we find ourselves, we can help bring ourselves back to a positive, happy condition. To quote Dr Bach, 'There is no true healing unless there is a change in outlook, peace of mind and inner happiness.' The remedies set out to help you make that change.

I have found them great healing tools, as they have a subtle but powerful effect on the personality. I have selected a few which may help you heal the aspects of your personality and behaviour that may be spoiling your relationships:

- ✧ **Crab Apple** to help with suffering of current or past abuse, self-hatred and sense of uncleanliness
- ✧ **Holly** for jealousy
- ✧ **Beech** for intolerance
- ✧ **Honeysuckle** for living in the past
- ✧ **Mimulus** for fear of abandonment
- ✧ **Centaury** if you are easily dominated
- ✧ **Chestnut Bud** to break patterns
- ✧ **Red Chestnut** if you are over-protective and fearful
- ✧ **Vine** if you are too controlling

There are a number of practitioners and therapists who specialise in the use of these remedies and you might find it helpful to visit one. Otherwise you can find information about them via the internet (see the Contacts section at the end of the book), and they are readily available in many chemists, including Boots. For those of you living in South America, Australia, New Zealand and southern Africa, there is a similar range of remedies called Australian Bush Flower Remedies, created for those living in the southern hemisphere.

Be kind to one another

IMPROVING YOUR RELATIONSHIP

How can you make your close relationships more loving and fulfilling? Let's take a look at some of the things that go wrong even in the best relationship and what you can do to revitalise a flagging relationship or improve a good one. Can a change of perspective and attitude help? Here are some general tips that I have drawn from my own experience of two marriages and from the observations of people I have helped.

LIFE GETS IN THE WAY

The words 'I will love you for ever and ever' are said with sincerity and feeling. So why is it that so many marriages fall by the wayside and fail to make ten years, let alone 'for ever'? Most marriages start with the very best of intentions. We are in love and loving, we do the best we can for our partners and we are tender, thoughtful and caring. But somewhere along the way the magic fades, and there are less and less of those romantic and tender moments that brought us such happiness in the early days. We seem to become thoughtless of each other; arguments and tetchiness creep in and become the norm.

You haven't failed if your marriage has faltered and struggled, for the romantic love of courtship soon gets beaten up by the everyday challenges of life. Financial worries, sleepless nights and other consequences of having children, problems with in-laws, cramped living conditions, work problems – all put a tremendous strain on us as individuals, and consequently on our marriages. It is easy to be loving and tender all the time in the first flush of romance – it's like living on a paradise island. But a deeper love – a tolerant,

Give each other space to be different

understanding, mature love – is needed in the reality of life. So let's consider what you can do to bring back that special relationship you had when you were first married, adding it to the wisdom that comes when you have lived in the reality of your everyday lives together.

PACKAGE DEAL

My husband is a strong character; single-minded, workaholic and not always an easy man. Like all of us, he has his faults and these have included very, very late nights, a tendency to dominate conversations and lack of interest in our domestic life. However, he is generous to a fault, softhearted, loving, kind and a brilliant provider. I soon realised in our marriage that I would never change him, and why should I? I would hate someone to try and change me. How dreadful to be bossed and bullied to change something as fundamental as one's own character. How invasive and awful would that be?

No, changing your partner is not an option in marriage as far as I'm concerned. So the other option is to accept. I decided to take my husband as a package deal – some bits are good and some not so good, but the good is far greater than the not so good! You are bound to find some of your partner's habits, attitudes and behaviour an irritation – if not a challenge – but try to see the bigger picture, try not to change them by nagging.

When I asked my friends about the things that irritated them about their partners, I was given quite a list – with snoring at the top! Their responses also included untidiness, being tied to the TV, being too laid back or too controlling, slamming the front door, fidgeting, not listening, fussing over trivia. Someone even cited too much sex, though that was

Laugh together

balanced out by a couple of men who felt a little deprived in that department.

None of these irritations or quirks have proved to be marriage breakers – they have all been tolerated and absorbed into happy marriages. So basically it's a case of learning tolerance and letting those habits, characteristics and actions of your partner that irritate you go over your head. Say what you feel about them – gently. And when they get a bit much, put yourself in a bubble. Literally visualise yourself in a bubble that insulates you from the more irritating aspects of your partner's behaviour.

DON'T MAKE A DRAMA

Don't blow things out of proportion. As the saying goes, 'Don't sweat the little stuff.' Save your strong words and emotions for when there is a serious event, and let minor disagreements slide by. I know some people who live on adrenaline and enjoy the dramas in their life, but they are exhausting for everyone. Nothing drains your energy more than emotional upset; my advice is to go for the peaceful option whenever you can.

I don't see anything wrong with giving in to an argument either – especially if it's just a difference of opinion. What does it matter? If it's not a life and death situation then let it go. The argument itself can cause more damage to your relationship than the issue that is being debated. Be big and capitulate: 'OK, you're right, no problem.' You may know that you are right, but what does it harm? Only your ego.

Be honest with each other without being hurtful

ENJOY THE DIFFERENCES

Remember, men and women do have different perspectives on life. Generally men are reluctant to ask for directions, can't find things that are under their noses, don't like shopping and flick channels. Women generally don't like Sunday TV football, eating or drinking out of a tin, or thirty-second telephone conversations! We enjoy different pastimes and different approaches to life, and as individuals we make different choices too. Try to enjoy the differences rather than niggle at them.

Tolerance is one of the basic keys to a happy marriage. Try laughing at these differences rather than attempting to change them. When the sport is on, my friends and I get a chance to read our books or work on the computer; we have maps and SatNav to find our way when travelling; we enjoy the freedom of shopping with girlfriends. Turn the differences around to your advantage and make the most of them, for they won't go away! Remember too that the differences make your relationship unique and fun – how boring it would be to live with a carbon copy of yourself.

Common ground

It's a good idea to develop your own interests and have some time for yourself, but it's important to have some shared interests too, that you can share outside of your working time. If you don't have a common pastime already, find something that you could both enjoy. Sue – a fifty-something lady I know – and her husband have taken up jive classes, which have become the highlight of a hectic and busy lifestyle for both of them.

Don't let things get bottled up

SUPPORT

One way to show your love is to always, always support each other in public. Whenever your partner is challenged by work issues, disputes with neighbours or arguments with other family members, showing support and belief can create tremendous bonds of love. Those acts of kindness and support when times get tough will always be remembered, so use the opportunity of any adversity in your lives to build the deep bonds that will take you the whole distance.

Try not to argue in front of children and friends, for it is not only embarrassing to be drawn into other people's disputes but it can also drive a wedge between you and your friends. Children especially get hurt when asked to take sides or hear their parents arguing. They tend to internalise the discord and can often blame themselves for antagonism and disagreements between their parents.

Praise

I think it's so important to compliment each other and lift each other up whenever you can. One can easily fall into habits such as picking up on all your partner's tiniest failings and generally talking down to them. I cringe when I hear someone mocking or dismissing their partner; it's so degrading and very damaging for self-esteem.

If one member of a partnership suffers from low self-esteem then the energies of the relationship will suffer. So it's far more beneficial for both of you if you lift each other up, praise and pass positive comments. All of us have faults, all of us find some things hard to manage. If we are ridiculed every time we make a mistake, we soon lose confidence. On a practical level this can create withdrawal symptoms or bring out defensively aggressive responses which result in further

Try to see things from the other's point of view

disharmony. There is no doubt that you get the best out of your partner if you are supportive and encouraging. I recently read an amusing article about a woman who adopted techniques used by animal trainers in order to train her husband out of his irritating habits! She praised him whenever he picked up his dirty clothes, arrived on time and shaved and ignored him whenever he caused a commotion through the house whenever he lost his temper. She neither nagged him or joined in the fuss. He soon quietened down and gradually she noticed he shaved more, picked up his clothes and his time keeping improved! I wonder if she fed him dog treats as well!

TALK, TALK, TALK AND TALK AGAIN

Practise sharing your emotions; tell your partner what you need and what you feel, for this can prevent misunderstandings. I have heard so many times 'I don't know what I've done to upset her/him.' If you don't tell your partner what they have done to upset you, they will be very confused about their next move. If your partner is slow to show his or her feelings, be a role model yourself and discuss the need to communicate. It's far easier to discuss problems away from the domestic scene, so a trip to a pub, a meal together, a walk can all give you the opportunity to talk situations through without distractions.

Make sure you have personal time together each week where you get away from the children, away from family and friends – time dedicated to the two of you. Weekend breaks are excellent for bonding and sharing. Two-way, balanced communication is a must for a good relationship. It's imperative to say what you feel even if you don't think the other person is either interested or understanding – once

Remember to have fun

you stop talking, the relationship will stop flourishing. And remember to keep on telling your partner how much you love them – you can never overuse the words 'I LOVE YOU'.

MAKE AN EFFORT

In our everyday lives we can be so pressed for time that we start to forget the little things we did for and to each other in the early, romantic days. These have to be worked at a little more when the baby's nappy needs changing, when there is a bus to catch, when the dinner needs cooking. However, it doesn't take a moment to rub a back, touch an arm, blow a kiss or squeeze a hand, and these acts can make a huge difference. If you have a little longer to spare, remember the favourite chocolate, pot noodle or flowers and drop them into the shopping basket. Don't just leave it to Valentine's day to buy a surprise present.

Dress to impress

My grandmother had a saying: 'You dress to catch a man, dress to keep him.' This might sound a little old-fashioned, but the sentiment still holds true. And of course it goes for guys as well as girls – we like to be wooed and courted by a smart-looking guy! It shows that you care, and it shows a respect for your partner to make an effort to look your best – so girls, allow time for relaxing in your trackie, but also wow him sometimes with something stunning. Which in turn can lead on to . . .

Essential sex

It's also essential to find time for sex. When you are in your teens and twenties that sounds like a preposterous

Enjoy, compromise and really work at your relationships

thought – 'Find time for sex? Why, I think of nothing else!' – especially if you are a testosterone-filled young man! However, if you are over thirty and have spent more than five years with your partner you may be finding that sex has become a less common event. After fifty you may be saving it for special occasions and holidays. It's worth making an effort, as you will be delighted with the experience once you get going. Not only is it a great sensual experience, but it's a great way of letting go tensions, losing yourself, even if momentarily. And, of course, it is the ultimate bonding with your partner.

VALUING YOUR RELATIONSHIP

The love that takes you all the way – that keeps you together and brings happiness to both of your lives – is the love that comes with sharing your lives, both the challenges and the good times. This is a more valuable and treasured love than the passion and ecstasy of the first months when you are floating in a miasma of pink cloud. If you are married I am sure you know and understand each other far better now than you did when you first married, and consequently you can make each other happier now too. So value what you have now, but remember that creating a romantic moment or two will give you the best of both worlds.

It is important from both a spiritual and practical perspective to value and appreciate what you have. The saying 'Use it or lose it' is most frequently used with regard to skills and gifts, but I think it's equally important to treasure and value our blessings, and a good marriage is a blessing. If you have a good partnership and want to develop it into a brilliant one, it may now be an appropriate time to acknowledge what you already have. So, let's look at appreciation, not only

Remember, nobody is perfect and the grass isn't always greener

of your partner but of the experience of being together and what that offers you.

I asked several friends and colleagues who enjoy flourishing, long-term relationships, 'What do you value most in your relationship?' Here are some of their responses. See if any relate to your situation and then write your own answer to the question.

✧ 'The level of trust and communication that we have with each other.'

✧ 'I am so lucky. You can have all the love in the world, but if you don't have unconditional trust, you have nothing.'

✧ 'A shared sense of humour, facing life together, trying to make sense of daily life, little things that my partner does . . . and that I can do for him. An anchor in a crazy world.'

✧ 'Integrity and trust, honesty and openness, mutual respect. We love each other so much that if we see a problem we talk it through rather than hurt each other.'

✧ 'Our openness to talk about anything and everything. A deep love and understanding of each other which has developed as we have been willing to go there with issues, and be vulnerable.'

THE SECRETS OF A SUCCESSFUL MARRIAGE

I also asked these couples, 'What advice would you give to a young couple just starting out together?' Some of their answers are given below. You may like to ask friends of yours who are in long-term and successful marriages the same question.

Do what you think is right and not what other people think is right

✧ 'Communicate, communicate, communicate. I feel it is so important to communicate what one is feeling. If your partner has a habit, for example, that drives you insane, you need to communicate this with your partner so that a more harmonious relationship can develop. I feel it is necessary to be honest and honour oneself and one's partner.'

✧ 'Be very clear on your priorities. What really matters most in your life? Know that your relationship will have ups and downs – it's just not possible to keep up that white hot passion indefinitely. Treat your partner the way YOU would like to be treated.'

✧ 'Don't be ashamed to show your feelings. Show your love and say "I love you" as often as you can.'

✧ 'Make sure your relationship is based on real friendship and understanding as well as love and passion – take the time to discover and accept each other's personalities, attitudes, morals, good and bad habits, baggage from the past, hopes and dreams for the future. They can differ widely from your own and will change with time, but that doesn't matter as you are not looking for a person exactly like yourself. However, understanding them, warts and all, and really LIKING your partner as well as LOVING him or her makes a firm basis for starting out on a life together.'

✧ 'Find someone you respect and admire so that when the hot passion subsides you still have a great friend and companion.' (She then added, 'Of course, a young couple won't understand this as they will be convinced the passion will never die!')

Never go to bed without being at peace with each other

✧ 'Remember the person is often reflecting aspects of you that you haven't yet loved, acknowledged or accepted. And the more you accept and love them for who they are, the more you love and accept yourself.'

This is just a sample of the responses, but the message that comes through loud and clear is that *communication and tolerance* are essential in a successful relationship. I also asked these people what they would like to change in their relationship, and – apart from those who would like their partner to stop snoring – what they said most often was that they would like more time together. I thought it was lovely that after twenty years and more together they still wanted to be in each other's company. Wonderful!

Finally, as we are focusing on improving relationships, let's see what people who have been together for years give as the reason for their success:

✧ 'Ability to communicate and express myself, acceptance of the other person as he is, not trying to change him.'

✧ 'Open and frequent communication; allowing each other space when needed without losing a close bond to each other; respecting the other for who they are without trying to change them, not trying to impose my own thinking or value system on her.'

✧ 'Although it's not always easy, one needs to learn to give and take as well as being tolerant.'

✧ 'True friendship, love, respect and easy compromise – he is such a lovely person. We value each other, acknowledging the little foibles, and basically both spend our days trying to make the other as happy as possible.'

Be kind to one another

GETTING ALONG BETTER WITH YOURSELF

Every problem you have with others reflects a problem you have with yourself. When you are irritated with yourself – running late, mislaying things, and so on – do you tend to snap at your nearest and dearest and pick on them? We often find faults in others that are actually aspects of ourselves we feel vulnerable about. Our self-criticisms are mirrored out to others.

When you are comfortable with yourself, when you have learnt to be tolerant and understanding of yourself, to be happy with who you are, when you have healed your inner wounds, then you will find it easier to live with others. You will also find that as you heal yourself, so you will attract others who are balanced and whole. We either tend to attract those into our lives who balance who we are, bringing to the partnership strengths where we ourselves have weaknesses; or, following the rule that like attracts like, we draw to ourselves people who have similar strengths and weaknesses, wounds or needs.

I know that I have learnt from my husband and seen in him strengths that I would like to aspire to. His ability to be calm and grounded when chaos reigns, his immense generosity, his ability in business to make balanced decisions, his trust in his own intuition and inner guidance and his discernment, his business sense have all either inspired me to grow my own strength in these areas or have given me the sense to leave certain areas of our life to him to manage! Throughout our time together I have continuously looked to heal those aspects of myself that are troubled with anxiety or guilt and as I have healed and learnt to know myself better so our relationship has developed and strengthened

Give each other space to be different

and our love has flourished. I have learnt what parts to leave alone and what parts to work on and grow; developing my strengths; accepting most of my weaknesses and healing my anxieties. We can all find aspects of ourselves that we need to heal – it's an ongoing process. So to help improve our personal relationships, especially relationships with those closest to us, it's beneficial to constantly look for signs that indicate that we may need healing.

Here are just some clues to hidden anxieties, scars and wounds that you may need to address:

✧ insecurity – anxiety about being alone, fear of the dark

✧ fear of new situations – reluctance to join clubs and socialise

✧ shyness with people – fear of meeting new people, speaking out

✧ lack of confidence – anxiety about trying in case of failure

✧ self-dislike – self-abuse, low self-esteem, lack of belief in self

✧ bubbling anger and resentment – sudden outbursts set off by minor situations

Work on letting go, forgiving and moving on from the past traumas that caused these anxieties and negative attitudes about yourself. Use the exercises that we have covered in this book to detach from past pain. Note the way your emotions are talking to you – listen to your feelings. When making decisions and choices, check what you feel like inside. Do you feel strong or nervous? Learn to understand what your feelings are saying to you. Listen to your own feelings rather than the advice of others, and trust that you do know what is good and right for you. Base your choices on these feelings and you will start to move in a positive direction. Once your heart opens, you will have access to the energy of love that you need for your healing.

Keep focused on:

✧ appreciating yourself

✧ respecting yourself

✧ being kind to yourself

✧ giving time to yourself

✧ being tolerant of yourself

✧ praising yourself

✧ forgiving yourself

✧ LOVING yourself

Treat your body well, as this sends a strong symbolic message to the holistic you. And as you feed yourself good, healthy food, give your body plenty of exercise, take time to relax, have time to play and so on, you will find that your total wellbeing and your capacity for love and happiness will increase. This in turn will encourage success and more love in your relationships.

I hope some of this chapter will press buttons for you, enabling you to shift your perception of your marriage and partner,

Be honest with each other without being hurtful

change your attitude in some way, alter your expectations, guide you to healing your relationship. In fact a great deal of what I have said applies not only to your relationship with your love but also to your relationships with family and friends, even with work colleagues.

Keep working on the exercises and processes in this book to give momentum to the cycle of love. As your heart opens and you work on your own issues, healing your heart, letting go attachments to past hurt and loving more unconditionally, so you will find that you attract more love into your life and your relationships will improve. As your relationships improve you will find it easier to be more loving; in turn, even more love will come back into your life, making you happier still. And so this uplifting cycle of love will continue.

Don't let things get bottled up

TEN

Attracting New Love

Finally, for those of you who do not have a serious relationship, let's look at how you can find new love. As your heart is opening to receive love, so we need to deal with the practical aspects of attracting and finding love.

ACTIVATING THE LAWS OF ATTRACTION AND CREATION

Through the exercises in this book you will have opened your heart and begun to heal your wounds. You may have felt some reaction in your chest, such as tension and tightening, you may have felt some shooting sensations or even a slight discomfort. All these are signs that your heart is opening and you are becoming more 'available' to love energy.

As you work on being more unconditional with your own loving, so you will be setting in action the spiritual law of attraction which draws similar energy forces together. You have the ability to create what you wish and desire. To tap into this ability, simply focus on your needs and hold a clear picture of what you wish to manifest in your life – more

Attract love that supports not detracts

love, new love, improved love, abundance and prosperity, support and friendship – and it will happen, for this is the law of creation. Your barriers are coming down now and with your newly opened heart ready to receive, there is nothing to stop you receiving the love you desire. Although love comes in many forms, let's first take a look at your romantic love life.

NEVER GIVE UP

You may be feeling a little despondent about your love life or having a tough time being single; even worrying whether you will ever meet that Mr or Mrs Right. Don't despair. It's never too late to meet love. I have a friend whose aunt has just met a man and fallen in love, and she is in her eighties. I recently visited South Africa and met a friend who has been single ever since I met him fifteen years ago. He was looking absolutely brilliant. New haircut, trendy clothes and a twinkle in his eye – yes, after many years alone he had met a great girl and was deeply, deeply in love. I was so happy for him. He must have waited over twenty years to meet this girl.

Of course, there are lots of people who actually prefer to live alone, and quite honestly there have been times in my life when I could have said that there are many benefits to such a way of living. You certainly don't have to worry about pleasing another and you can have a very satisfying and fulfilling life – as long as you find love somewhere, whether it be from your spiritual connections, from friends or from family.

However, if you feel that you need the comfort, companionship and deeper love of a full-time partner, then don't despair if you haven't met anyone so far who fits the bill.

Attract love that respects not puts you down

You never know when the right person may slip around the corner. Then bang! you're hooked. This is how it worked out for me.

My story

When I was in my twenties and coming to the end of my first marriage, I fell deeply in love with one of my work colleagues. His marriage was also failing and his wife had taken a boyfriend – which, you might say, rather left him surplus to requirements. So I left my husband. It was an extremely traumatic and sad experience, and anyone who has been through something similar will know that the thrill of meeting the great love of your life cannot be enjoyed fully if your ex-partner suffers. It's a very difficult and challenging time, and my sympathies are with anyone making the decision whether to stay, unfulfilled and unhappy, or leave, hurting a partner and worse still children.

Fortunately I had no children and we moved in together. But he was going through the challenge of leaving two small children; eventually, after a few weeks of happy togetherness, the pull of his little ones was too much and he left me to go back to them. I was absolutely devastated. I still remember the colour leaving my world the day he left.

I threw myself into my work and for the next thirteen years became a dedicated career woman, travelling the world selling computers. I had a fascinating and challenging job and naturally met many men on the way, although no one stole my heart – which was just as well in the light of future events! I moved to South Africa and worked there for four years. Again, despite the lure of a few hunky men I kept my heart intact. I enjoyed my life to the full. I had a fun group of girlfriends and a tremendous social life and I had learned to love being single.

Attract love that comes with tenderness

However, one of my girlfriends, who was addicted to fortune tellers, rang me one day to tell me she had found an amazing Lebanese psychic and asked me to come with her for a reading. Just for fun, I agreed. The psychic made her connection by holding my watch and predicted that in the next few weeks I would meet a businessman from overseas; a big man, a strong man, older than me. He would sweep me off my feet and take me abroad, we would marry within a year and travel around the world. She saw a very happy and strong marriage and even gave me the date by which I would meet him. Wow. I must admit her message left me quite excited and expectant. My intention of staying single was starting to waver.

A few evenings later I received a phone call from an old friend. Tony, my lover from my twenties, was coming to South Africa on a business visit and had bumped into a mutual friend who had passed him my telephone number. We arranged to meet up. But my immediate thought was that the weekend he had chosen was the final date for me to meet my Mr Wonderful. How was that going to work now that I had Tony to entertain? I was delighted to be seeing him, but surely he would ruin my chances!

In short, we met up and we fell into each other's arms. We spent the entire weekend catching up with our news and found that we were now both single and unattached. However, it wasn't until we were saying our farewells at the airport that we realised we had fallen in love again. It was an extremely emotional parting, and having a man in my life once more suddenly felt like a great idea.

I went to see the fortune teller the next week. As I walked in the door, she said, 'I see you've met him then.'

'Yes,' I replied, 'but he's younger than me.'

Quick as a flash she retorted, 'Well, he looks older than

Attract love that comes with respect

you.' Which he did – he was completely grey, even though he was only 37 at the time. (He doesn't like me telling people about that!)

Every night he rang me from wherever in the world he was. Within months I left South Africa and returned to England to be married. He took me on a trip round the world for our honeymoon, and in every way he has fulfilled the fortune teller's prophetic words.

KEEP AN OPEN MIND

So the moral of the story is that you never know how or when you will meet love. As an old lady once told me, 'Keep your eyes open all the time, my dear. Even when dancing, look over his shoulder – you never know who will walk into the room.' A bit over the top maybe, but a sensible message. I say 'Keep your doors and windows open – keep an open mind and don't dismiss someone just because they don't look right to you – look beneath the surface, for there could be a golden nugget hidden inside.'

I know some women who instantly dismiss men who don't match their ideal. It doesn't pay to have too strong a blueprint in your mind of the person you want to meet. This is for the fellas too. I know of lots of men who have a Pamela Anderson image firmly fixed in their heads. Although this might make their daydreams exciting, it doesn't often work out in real life.

A group of single friends took part in a workshop to prepare them for meeting their ideal man. One of the exercises they were given required them to write down all that they wanted from the man of their dreams. Most of them had had bad experiences in the past, so I presume the workshop leader was encouraging them to be selective in choosing

Attract love that ennobles you

a partner next time. Anyway, my friend Suzie became completely carried away with the exercise. She wrote a very long and very detailed list of what she wanted in her man. She even gave a graphic description of his looks and his fashion preferences.

We all had a laugh and told her never in a million years – get real! However, soon afterwards she started a relationship with a man on the internet. And, believe it or not, he really did seem to have all the qualities she was looking for – at least on the intellectual, emotional and interest levels. Finally the day came for her to meet him. And yes, he was a good-looking guy. But there was one thing missing – his hair. He was bald. You see, she had forgotten to mention his hair in her list!

They did have a relationship, but it didn't last – maybe her expectations were a little too high. But we all had a good laugh at her expense. So, don't be too detailed in your list – or at least if you must get down to details, do remember to give your partner some hair!

IT'S IN THE STARS

Before we move on I would like to share a few thoughts about fortune tellers, mediums, tarot readers and channels who pass messages from spiritual guides. As I have said, I have visited them many times over the years out of a mixture of fun and curiosity – and, I guess, at times out of need. I have been to all sorts. In recent years I have still consulted the occasional psychic reader but I prefer to refer to a good channel.

As I described earlier, a channel is someone who allows an evolved being in spirit to speak through them. The best do this without stagecraft and performance, simply allowing the spirit to use their voice to communicate their messages.

Attract love that's fun

The accuracy and substance of the information coming through seems to depend on the purity of the channel. By purity I mean the level of spiritual attainment the channel has reached and their lack of ego. A good channel will be sincerely interested in helping their client.

Through this method you can speak directly to an angelic being, a spiritual guide or an Ascended Master and can ask specific questions. An Ascended Master like John the Beloved, my favourite channel, is an evolved being who has lived on earth, reached a level of spiritual evolution where it is no longer necessary for them to return to Earth for development purposes, and who now holds the intention of helping mankind from the realms of spirit. Ascended Masters are all-knowing and all-understanding and they work completely from love. They have a wisdom and compassion that is seldom found on Earth.

Destiny or will

Now I am often asked a question that relates to all reading of the future, whether it be from a tarot reading, tea leaves or Ascended Master. 'Is it a good idea to know about the future? For if you know what is supposed to happen to you, do you try to make it happen?' It's a good question and one that I have thought about a lot. Another question I am asked is 'What is the point of having readings anyway? Is our destiny laid out before we are born, as many think, or do we make our own fate as we live our lives?' I have taught many workshops covering the subject of manifestation – creating your own life, your own luck, your own future. How does that sit with the fact that fortune tellers, like the one who told me of my future with Tony, can tell us what is going to happen in our lives?

This is how I believe it works. Before you are born you

Attract love that sees the light inside you

plan your future life. You have an immense amount of spiritual help in the realms where your soul resides before your birth. With the assistance of spiritual elders and guides you plan a life that will challenge you where needed, teach you the lessons you wish to learn, give you contact with those who you need to help, allow you to give the service that you desire. Your ultimate aim is to develop spiritually towards an evolvement of being that eventually means you can leave the cycle of birth and death and move to higher, more spiritual realms.

So you make a plan of your mission and purpose for the life ahead. You discuss this with your soul group members – soul groups are those souls with whom you return to Earth frequently; they will be mostly family members and close friends. Although sometimes they will challenge you, most often they are there giving you love and support, depending on the role they have agreed to play. Now you are ready to come into the dense form that is our body for the duration of our life on Earth. Oh yes, you also have plans for your death – exit plans, I call them. These plans will be based on the purpose of that lifetime. If you come for service, you may need just a few years to share a portion of someone's life. Or you may come to learn about some form of suffering, in which case you may die young of a disease. There will be a number of exit points when you may be able to leave. It will be your choice when you are here which one you finally use.

So the plan is made. But it is *not* cast in stone! When you get going with your life you may decide to change your destiny, you may decide that you do not wish to leave at the first planned exit point. Or you may find that life is more overwhelming and challenging than you anticipated and that you just can't manage.

Your personality and character are made up of your genetic

inheritance – attributes, attitudes and tendencies inherited from your parents – and your soul characteristics, which are a direct result of your experiences thus far in your soul's journey through the cycles of life and death. So a soul can pick up an anxious disposition from its parents and have to cope with this, even struggle to overcome nervous tendencies. Of course, this will end up making a stronger individual. But it can be a severe challenge. Some don't make it and bail out through suicide or accident. They regroup and have a healing in the spirit realms before making a new journey with a slightly modified agenda. Now, how does this fit with our psychic readings?

Psychics may have the ability to tap into your plan directly, but most often they communicate with those in the spirit realms who have a full understanding of your purpose and proposed destiny. They will be informed if someone is meant to meet up with you and make a partnership; they can see if you are likely to have any major illnesses; they can see most of the major events that are due to come along. However, I have found that there are some things they do not see and are not told by our spiritual friends. It's not that they are deliberately misled by our spirit guides, but the fact is that if we knew about certain future events we would change our attitude, stop acting naturally. The knowledge might even create some fear within us that would affect the way we approach these events. So you won't necessarily be told everything – sorry!

WILL POWER FOR CHOICES

When we are born on Earth we have a fundamental gift which gives us great power, one which I believe we do not use to its maximum effect. That is our freedom of choice – our will. You have the ability to create what you want and to overcome much of your destined path, if you so wish. You can draw towards you positive situations and people and you can walk the path of your choice. This free spirit that is within all of us is a mixed blessing, of course, for you can choose to do things that are not necessarily in your best interest. And you can end up spending time in your life with people who may be politely called a challenge. I have found the best route is to follow what feels good in my heart and listen to my intuition.

Back to the main subject of this book – healing and opening your heart. There is no doubt that the healthier and more balanced your heart centre is, the easier it is to be in touch with your intuition, which is the direct communication with your soul and with your spirit guides. So, yes, you have a destiny planned out, but you are in a position to re-direct it and rewrite the script if you wish.

The full implications of this, of course, you will not find out until you get back into spirit and review your life, see how your choices and decisions have affected the outcome of your life. But if you follow my advice you will always do what feels good and right for you deep inside, without any niggling doubts. All of which means that there are things you can do to meet the woman or man of your dreams; put yourself into Cupid's way and go and look for someone to share your life. He or she is unlikely to come knocking on the door, so I suggest you make your own opportunities.

MEETING A NEW PARTNER

It's essential that you get out and about. Even if you don't meet Mr or Mrs Right straight away, you can have fun and

Attract love that makes you feel warm

it will be good practice for when someone does come along. You can get rusty if you don't commingle for some time.

MAISIE

A friend of mine, Maisie, had a very deep and serious relationship in her twenties that didn't work out – it ended with many tears and heartbreak. Since that time she has retreated more and more behind her barriers. In her early forties she suddenly realised that time was ticking on and she felt the need and desire to have a close relationship again. It's been difficult for her to change the reclusive habits and attitudes she's developed over the years in which she has been running from the closeness of a relationship. She has spent time now working on her heart healing and I notice that gradually she is allowing herself to open up. I am absolutely sure that before long she will meet someone special. As she lets down her internal barriers and moves in the places where she can meet men, her natural beauty and character will attract someone to her side.

There are a number of ways to meet a lover. I found it interesting to see how my friends had met their long-term partners:

✧ in a restaurant

✧ during a seminar and retreat

✧ at work in an airport

✧ at the amateur dramatic society

✧ introduced by a friend

Attract love that's light

✧ at a festival

✧ at a dance

✧ at a friend's home

✧ in a pub

✧ at the leisure centre

All of these were out and about – so join a club, evening class, gym or whatever interests you, as you are more likely to find a like-minded soul that way.

SINGLES CLUBS

Singles clubs are great, as they have already sorted out the likely candidates for you. There are now dating clubs or evenings. Some of my friends have tried speed dating, where you meet a whole group of people in one night – spending just ten or twenty minutes with each one before moving on to the next. Fast-track work!

DATING AGENCIES

Quite a number of my single friends have made great connections through dating agencies. One friend in particular is having a fabulous time with guys she has met through internet dating agencies. She is a busy woman and the agency selects those who have similar interests and expectations to her, saving her time and disappointment. The trick is not to feel ashamed or embarrassed about using these services – they are quite cool these days!

Attract love that gives you wings

THROUGH FRIENDS

If you feel it's time to meet a new partner, ask your friends to help – most people love to be matchmakers. Through work colleagues, family and friends, there is likely to be someone who is free.

PINK CHAMPAGNE

Before I met Tony I belonged to a 'Thursday' club. That was great fun. Every Thursday a number of single friends would meet and drink pink sparkling wine (our budget didn't run to real champagne!) in pink glasses – very girly. We then went out for a meal to a fun restaurant and from there, those who were so inclined went dancing at a club. Often Thursday night is singles night in clubs. We were a group of anything from four to ten and we had a wonderful time. There was always lots of laughter. We would meet up with groups of men and sometimes one of us would find a match.

Because we were there to enjoy ourselves we seemed to attract fun guys, and as we were a largish group no one felt left out. This is a great way to get out and about without feeling conspicuous or obvious and it suited even the shyest of our group. Several of us were nursing sore hearts from cheating husbands, and yet they felt happy about mixing again this way. Clubbing with friends is easy these days. Every town has a proliferation of clubs where you can mix with and meet people of all ages.

ATTRACTING THE RIGHT PERSON

Working through this book will set you off in the right direction. If you have worked on opening your heart and healing the blocks between you and love, then there is no reason for you not to attract someone who will love you. Hold the intention to attract the right kind of love and the right kind of people. But try not to be too keen! Neediness is a deterrent. If a guy tries too hard and seems desperate he will immediately put a girl off, and vice versa. And remember, each one of us is unique and has different tastes in partners, so never be put off by the comments of your friends and family – it's what you want that matters. So be honest with yourself and give it a go.

SOUL MATES

I'm often asked questions about soul mates: 'Should I wait for my soul mate? Will I know him when he arrives?' Soul mates are from your soul group, a collection of souls who have shared previous lifetimes with you. Soul mates don't necessarily have to be lovers. They can support you with your life's purpose and help you to face your life challenges as friends, family members or even work colleagues.

They sometimes create challenges for you by pressing your buttons and creating an environment to test and try you. This is done with the intention of giving you an opportunity to break patterns of behaviour or attitudes that are haunting you from lifetime to lifetime; offering you the chance to grow and evolve. You grow through overcoming adversity and those closest to us are best situated to give you such challenges. A soul mate may be a boss who gives you a hard time, a difficult neighbour, a husband in a seemingly

Attract love that allows you a voice

disastrous marriage, or a mother who tries to control you. And so on.

There is a story about a man who became a beggar. He would sit outside a successful businessman's office, testing him every day to see if he would help him. The vagrant was a soul mate of the rich man and was testing two things – whether the businessman would be able to recognise a soul mate through the barrier of his wealth and different situation in life, and whether he still had an open heart and was able to be generous to someone in need. You'll be glad to know he did in fact assist his old soul friend. You never know where or when a soul mate may be helping you.

There may also be a soul mate you have loved deeply in many lifetimes, and who you have a life plan to meet up with and spend time with in this lifetime. As with my story about meeting my husband, it would seem that if you meet up with such a soul mate there is little chance that you will miss each other! The feelings of 'love at first sight' and 'we were made for each other' only touch the deep and overwhelming feelings of association and closeness, the warmth of coming home, that you feel when you meet.

However, if you lose such a lover there may well be other soul mates waiting to help you and share further time with you in your life. So don't feel that there is only one love for you. You may be passing by the opportunity to have a loving, fun relationship with someone who is waiting in the wings of your life.

LOVE IN MANY GUISES

All unconditional love will uplift and enlarge your life. It will stimulate you and give you inner satisfaction and fulfilment. A partner is only one source of love – don't disregard

Attract love that sits easily with you

or underrate the effect on your life of love from friends, family, co-workers and the people who share your life. If you love nature or animals you have another source of love. And finally remember that the most powerful, intense and totally unconditional love, a love that is also freely available, is the love from the Divine. You will find this love free and available. Just open your heart and see it. Hold it within you and connect with everything created – good books, music, plants, in fact the beauty of everything around you.

THE KEY

Lastly, remember that while your heart is closed love will be unable to come into your life. It will not batter down your door – this is something you will have to do for yourself. Keep up with the practices, exercises and meditations that we have gone through and gradually you will find that the past is healed and the door to your heart is open.

Remember the three spiritual laws that will help you:

✧ **The law of karma.** This is activated as you give love – what you give out comes back. The more you give love, the more love will come to you.

✧ **The law of attraction.** This is activated as you become more loving – things of like vibration are drawn to each other. As you change your energy vibration to the vibration of love, so you will attract those who have similar vibrations and are on your wavelength. Keep in mind that love comes in many forms. Being kind, thoughtful and gentle with yourself and others will change the vibration of your personal energy. As your personal self-esteem and

Attract love that makes you feel good about yourself

confidence grows, you will become lighter and radiate a loving essence that will attract more love towards you like a magnet.

✧ **The law of creation.** This will be activated as you visualise the love you wish to attract, draw up your list, hold the expectation and the intention of the form and style of love you desire. You create your desires. Be careful with this one!

Before I leave, let me remind you that the journey to a life filled with love can be a little turbulent at times. As you open you may find that occasionally your emotions go up and down. Don't worry about this. It's a natural reaction to the process of opening, the emotional and spiritual shift as your personal energy vibrations become lighter and more loving. After a few months of your heart opening, all will stabilise. You will start to wake to more days filled with the joy of life and fewer filled with its struggle.

So I have come to the end of this book. I hope that it has helped you to bring down some barriers, healed some wounds and aided you in finding more love. Remember love is the key to healing emotionally, spiritually and physically; it enables you to enjoy life to its fullest and to allow you to grow to your greatest potential. I wish you well in your search for love – it's all around you and can be found in the most unexpected places. So keep your eyes open and watch out for Cupid!

Love and blessings

Anne

Attract love that gives not takes

RESOURCES

CHANNELS AND HEALERS

Helen Barton channels John the Beloved, a spiritual adviser and teacher living in Australia who gives guidance on emotional and life issues.
Website: www.johnthebeloved.com
Email: insight2@bigpond.net.au
Tel: ++617 55 25 35 20

Lee Carroll channels Kryon
Website: www.kryon.com

Tom Kenyon, sound healer, channels the Hathors
Website: www.tomkenyon.com

Amanda King, holistic personal trainer
Email: amandapt@tiscali.co.uk
Tel: 079 662 29416

Claire Montanaro, spiritual teacher, counsellor and channel
Website: www.clairemontanaro.com.
Email: claire@clairemontanaro.com
Telephone readings: 01597 811 110

Janet Thompson, past life therapist and counsellor
Website: www.janetthompson.org.uk
Email: mailme@janetthompson.org

Sue Harper, counsellor and homeopath
Email: susanmharper@onetel.com

Channelling from Tobias
Website: www.crimsoncircle.com

AID AGENCIES
Dr Cary
A medical doctor who gave up his lucrative practice in Chicago to serve the world's poorest and most needy peoples. His work and writing are an inspiration to all and a testament to unconditional love. Visit his website to read about his medical missions in rural India, the Amazon, with Hmong refugees in Thailand, Tibetan refugees in Nepal, etc. His mission creates opportunities for others to have the privilege of giving.
Website: www.drcary.org

Free Tibet
Campaigns for the Tibetan people's right to determine their future
Website: www.freetibet.org

Twyman's Peace Organisation
Their goal is to help millions of people around the world enjoy the experience of deep inner peace.
Website: www.emissaryoflight.com

Kham Aid Agency

Provides education for Tibetan children and trains midwives and health care workers for Tibetan villages
Website: www.khamaid.org

SUPPORT ORGANISATIONS

Dating agencies:

uk.personals.yahoo.com
www.datingdirect.com
www.encounters.timesonline.co.uk – linked to the *Sunday Times*

Domestic abuse

In an emergency, you should call the police on 999 (minicom 0800 112 999). Domestic violence is treated very seriously by the police and the courts. You can also call the 24 Hour National Domestic Violence Helpline on 0808 2000 247.

Samaritans

UK charity offering support to people who are suicidal or despairing. They are on hand 24 hours a day, every day of the year.
Website: www.samaritans.org.uk
Email: jo@samaritans.org
Tel: 08457 909090

Victim Support

UK charity that helps victims of crime including rape
Website: www.victimsupport.org
Help line: 0845 3030 900

Women's Aid

Organisation giving help and assistance to women suffering domestic violence. They will give advice on refuge, legal rights, police protection, how you can protect your children, housing options, etc.

Website: www.womensaid.org.uk

Help line: 0808 2000 247

BOOKS

Sophy Burnham, *A Book of Angels*, Ballantine, 1990

A delightful introduction to the work of angels and a great insight into the angelic realms.

Alma Daniel, Timothy Wyllie & Andrew Ramer, *Ask Your Angels*, Piatkus, 1992

Great advice on how to connect to angels and to call upon them for help in your daily life.

Esther and Jerry Hicks, *Ask and It Is Given*, Hay House, 2005

Learn how to manifest your desires from guidance received from Esther's spiritual guide, Abraham.

Xinran, *Sky Burial*, Vintage, 2005

A truly amazing true story of a Chinese woman's 30-year search throughout Tibet for news of her husband, lost and presumed dead. An extraordinary story and a wonderful insight to life in Tibet.

ANNE'S SEMINARS

I give seminars around the world and a full schedule of my events can be found on my website, www.annejones.org. In relation to this book you may find the following workshop particularly helpful:

Healing Heart and Soul
A Seminar and Personal Integration
Opening Your Heart
A 3 hour seminar followed by a personal integration session. The seminar will be a group healing focused on opening the heart to receive the love you need to heal the imprints and wounds of the soul.

The personal one to one sessions will help clear karma and any blocks that prevent you receiving love and abundance, healing soul wounds and then integrate you to your Highest Self and the blueprint of your life that holds your purpose and soul intention.

Do you need it?

✧ Do you feel unfocused and unsure of the way ahead?

✧ Do you need more direction and clarity about your work?

✧ Do you feel blocked and unable to 'get going' with your life's work?

✧ Do you feel anxious and nervous without knowing the reason?

What can it do for you?

✧ Bring an inner peace and calm with a clearer focus of self.

✧ Help you to see the way ahead and clear the blocks to your potential

✧ Connect you to your Higher Self and your life blueprint

✧ Allow you to enjoy life and the richness of working through your highest essence – doing what you came to do!

For information and booking contact Brenda at sales@make-ripples.com or call 44 (0)1425 403228 or write to 21 Honey Lane, Burley, Ringwood, BH24 4EN, UK.

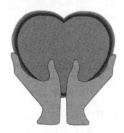

Hearts&Hands

Hearts and Hands is a non-profit-making organisation that is dedicated to spreading the use and understanding of natural energy healing.
We offer:

✧ workshops

✧ healing sessions

✧ spiritual counselling service with qualified counsellors

✧ a distance healing service.

If you would like to use one of these services or become a healer on our register please visit our website www.heartshands.org

R I P P L E

RIPPLE ENERGY THERAPY

www.make-ripples.com

To assist in spreading the energies of love and healing I have created Ripple, a small company based in the peace and tranquillity of the New Forest in the South West of England where we hand bottle organic essential oil blends for energy and emotional healing. Our range includes Anointing Oils, Rollerscents, Heart Balm and AromaMist sprays for clearing personal auras and rooms. I have also created a collection of silver jewellery using the symbols I use in my healing work.

Ripple energy therapy products that can be helpful with affairs of the heart:

◇ For healing wounds of the heart: Heart Balm lotion and Love anointing oil

◇ For releasing past attachments: Letting Go anointing oil

◇ To bring the energies of love to your home or work-space: Love and Nurture AromaMist

◇ To attract and give more love: Peace and Harmony silver pendant with rose quartz in the symbol of the everlasting flame.

All these products and my guided visualisation CDs are available on our website, www.make-ripples.com

For a brochure please contact us at info@make-ripples.com or write to Ripple UK Ltd, 21 Honey Lane, Burley, Hants, BH24 4EN, U.K.

We support a number of charities around the world including The Child Welfare Scheme in Nepal, Noah's Ark in South Africa and Women with Cancer in Malaysia.

INDEX

Note: page numbers in **bold** refer to diagrams.